Insider-Outsider Research in Qualitative Inquiry

Insider-Outsider Research in Qualitative Inquiry: New Perspectives on Method and Meaning explores the history, practice and particular benefits of conducting cultural research through a partnership of two researchers: one who is an insider to the culture under study and one who is an outsider. This book unpacks terminology around this type of research that has become outdated or cumbersome, looks at ethical issues and suggests specific methodological approaches. It also locates insider-outsider research, which is by its nature qualitative, in the wider research landscape. The authors specifically describe a researcher *partnership*, a relationship more intimate and fruitful than a team, much greater than the sum of its parts. Through their own nearly twenty-year research partnership and study of the Israeli Druze, the authors have developed mutual trust that has led to new depths of insight in understanding cultural codes and the meanings they embody. This, and the methods they use, will be illustrated through examples of some of their studies with the Israeli Druze.

A highly accessible guide, this book will be of interest to ethnographers and other qualitative researchers, both graduate students and researchers of all levels of experience.

Deborah Court is Associate Professor of Education at Bar-Ilan University and Academic Advisor at the Arab Academic College in Israel. With a background in cultural anthropology, her research centers on educational cultures, the nature of cultural knowledge, intercultural and interreligious understanding and qualitative research methodologies.

Randa Khair Abbas is Associate Professor, Academic Head and Rector of the Arab Academic College in Israel. Her research centers on Druze identity and the cultural, religious and family structures of the Druze community. She works also in women's rights, women's leadership and the advancement of Arab women in the professional landscape.

Insider-Outsider Research in Qualitative Inquiry

New Perspectives on Method and Meaning

Deborah Court and Randa Khair Abbas

Routledge
Taylor & Francis Group

LONDON AND NEW YORK

First published 2022
by Routledge
4 Park Square, Milton Park, Abingdon, Oxon OX14 4RN

and by Routledge
605 Third Avenue, New York, NY 10158

Routledge is an imprint of the Taylor & Francis Group, an informa business

© 2022 Deborah Court and Randa Khair Abbas

British Library Cataloguing-in-Publication Data
A catalogue record for this book is available from the British Library

Library of Congress Cataloging-in-Publication Data
A catalog record for this book has been requested

ISBN: 978-1-032-21486-3 (hbk)
ISBN: 978-1-032-21487-0 (pbk)
ISBN: 978-1-003-26862-8 (ebk)

DOI: 10.4324/9781003268628

Typeset in Times New Roman
by Apex CoVantage, LLC

Contents

Introduction   1

1   A conceptual and perceptual review of insider-
    outsider research   4

2   Our stories   14

3   Unearthing cultural codes: A visit to the graveyard   21

4   All in the family: Unraveling the strands of a
    crowded interview   29

5   Ethical issues in insider-outsider research and
    navigating the jargon jungle   37

6   What has gender got to do with it?   45

7   May God have mercy on this thing: Religious codes
    and women's struggle for fulfillment   57

8   New perspectives on method and meaning   69

    Index   79

Introduction

The year is 2003. The qualitative research methods class takes place at six in the evening. The forty or so students are tired. They are teachers, working all day and taking courses toward their master's degree in the evenings. They have children at home, lessons to prepare for school and essays to write for their graduate courses.

The lecturer is tired, too, after a long day and with a long drive home ahead of her, fighting traffic. But she loves her topic. Secretly, subversively, she feels like she is engaged in a kind of religious conversion process with her students. Qualitative research is in its infancy at this university and in this country. Statistics is king; all the students know, because they have learned it, that only quantitative research can produce valid, reliable knowledge. Only numbers can speak the truth, not words. Qualitative research can only describe, can only present soft things like feelings. It is, as one professor in this department has said, "Research for women – blah, blah, blah, blah, blah."

As the semester progresses, lights do go on in the eyes of no small number of the students. Understanding dawns: Yes, there *are* other kinds of knowledge, other kinds of data, other ways of arriving at new understanding of the human condition. Some remain unconverted to the end, but they are polite. And they are all tired.

It is hard for the instructor to learn the names of all these forty students. Forty is a lot of students for a qualitative methods class. And she has other classes, other groups of students. On this particular night, the class is especially sleepy, and perhaps it is for this reason that she notices, though not for the first time, the light in the eyes of one particular young woman, the rapt attention she pays, the intelligence of her shyly offered questions and comments. She asks this young woman to stay after class.

In later years, as they remember this night, Randa tells Deborah, "I couldn't understand why you wanted me to stay after class! What did I do wrong? I wondered."

DOI: 10.4324/9781003268628-1

Deborah asks Randa her name and whether she is doing a thesis or non-thesis master's degree. "Oh, non-thesis," Randa replies. Deborah thinks she recognizes her own past self in the self-effacing answer of the teacher who does not see herself as a legitimate academic and cannot imagine herself as a researcher.

"Why don't you do a thesis?" asks Deborah. "I will be your advisor." "A thesis? Me?" thinks Randa. And then, yes. Why not? Together they go to the appropriate department head, miraculously still in his office at this late hour, and fill out the paperwork.

And thus begins an almost (at the time of this writing) twenty-year relationship that begins as student and advisor, blossoms into a research partnership and deep friendship and culminates in Deborah working for Randa, who is now a professor heading a college. During many shared studies, Randa, the native Israeli Druze, and Deborah, the Canadian, Jewish immigrant to Israel, have delved into Druze identity, citizenship, religious and value orientations, leadership, the lives of women, child-rearing and education.

Clearly Randa is the insider and Deborah the outsider in all of these studies. But, as many writers have pointed out, insider and outsider are not black and white categories. We both trained as teachers before doing graduate degrees and becoming researchers. Schools are schools, everywhere, in so many ways. We share this background as educators. Studying a school, we are in some ways both insiders. We are both mothers. Studying families and child-rearing also bestows a level of insider status on us both. We will elaborate on the complex nature of insider and outsider status in chapter two.

We claim in this book to offer new insights into insider-outsider research. These new insights come from the intimacy of our research partnership, the two widely different worlds from which we come, the knowledge and experience we share and the many ways we have learned from and with each other. We will try, as we progress through this book, to tease out some of the subtleties of a research partnership like ours and to glean practical principles from them.

As with any intensive work, we have met methodological, analytical and ethical challenges and learning along the way. Each chapter in the book will describe challenges, learnings and insights and generate from these experiences guidelines that other research partnerships may find helpful. We specifically refer to ourselves not as a team but as a research *partnership*, a term that better captures the almost telepathic closeness that has both helped and hindered us.

In this brief volume, we will first survey the history of insider-outsider research. We will then tell our personal stories, because these are inextricably bound to the insights we gained, and the more generalized learnings and principles that we wish to share.

These stories will be followed by two chapters that provide case studies. In each of these, we will describe one study we conducted, relating to methods, dilemmas, data collection and analysis and insights we gained through working together.

Chapter five examines ethical issues related to power, authority, status and the many subtleties involved in insider-outsider partnerships, as well as the sometimes cumbersome vocabulary that has evolved in research discourse around these issues. We will attempt to unravel the continuing, little spoken of fact that in insider-outsider work, it is almost always the traditional or minority culture that the insider represents, and it is that traditional or minority culture that is studied. The outsider is usually from mainstream, Western academic culture. Western academic hegemony is still at work.

Chapter six looks closely at gender-matching and rapport in insider-outsider research, and chapter seven offers an additional case study. In the concluding chapter, we will tie together the insights accumulated throughout the book, in the hopes of providing, as the book's title promises, new perspectives on method and meaning.

We are glad that you, the reader, is sharing our story, and hope that you will take from this book new ideas for your own research journey.

1 A conceptual and perceptual review of insider-outsider research

First, a caveat. This chapter does not claim or aim to be a "review of the literature" on insider-outsider research. What we hope to do here is trace a modest, somewhat wandering but, we hope, coherent, path, through early anthropology (the general study of human society and culture) and ethnography (the method by which cultural anthropology is conducted; the study of specific cultures and societies), and then, more generally, into the social sciences, particularly education. In the various disciplines of the humanities, fieldwork is conducted to understand people, their lives, families, social structures, values, works, hopes and dreams, on the local level, in order (and this is always the challenge!) to arrive at some new "generalizable" understandings of the human condition. The path we will trace will bring us to these central questions: Who should conduct such fieldwork? Who is best placed to arrive at "true" knowledge? Participants in the culture, or those outside it? Each position carries potential insights, blinders and challenges.

Let us begin.

All stories must begin somewhere. Beginnings, of course, have their roots in previous beginnings. Every thinker or writer finds his or her roots in the thoughts and writings of those who went before. Any review of ideas, concepts and methods begins at a significant but inexact point. We could, in fact, begin in antiquity; people have always been interested in how "foreign" peoples live and have for many centuries written their observations of cultures they encountered on their travels. Marco Polo did this; Columbus did it; explorers and traders and wandering poets have encountered, described and tried to understand "foreign" cultures for centuries. Hodgen (1964) says that we can trace the foundational concepts of anthropology at least as far back as the sixteenth century, when exploration and trade were bringing about the meeting of cultures such as never before. Our review begins with Bronislaw Malinowski, who is widely considered to be the founder of social anthropology.

Before turning to the contributions of Malinowski to this discussion, though, we would be remiss if we did not devote a paragraph to the other

DOI: 10.4324/9781003268628-2

great early anthropologist, Franz Boas. Boas was born twenty-six years before Malinowski and was working before him, though they both died in 1942, researching and writing during the same period during the 1920s and 1930s. Boas, often called the father of American anthropology, was trained as a geographer. As a geographer he traveled to the frozen Canadian north to study the relationship between the physical environment and native Inuit migration patterns. This sparked his interest in the study of culture, and he embarked on several follow-up ethnographic field trips. He used the results of his ethnographic work, as well as studies of human skeletons from various cultures, to argue against the scientific racism that was dominant at the time. The Euro-centric beliefs of the time stated that cultures evolve through a series of predictable, hierarchical and physical stages and that European culture is the pinnacle of human culture. All "primitive" or Indigenous cultures are less advanced, lower on this hierarchical scale. Boas introduced the idea of cultural relativism that different cultures are different but equal and that people view other cultures through the lens of their own culture (Levy-Zumwalt 2019). This was an extremely important contribution, the beginning of the freeing of the anthropological mind. Understanding that Indigenous cultures are no less valuable, human and sophisticated than Western cultures also spelled the slow beginning of the end of the "history of exploitive research that contributed little to no benefit, or worse, research that caused damaging effects for Indigenous peoples and their communities" (Webster and John 2010, 175).

No doubt influenced by the older Boas, Malinowski brought to the young field of anthropology the understanding that culture can only be understood from the inside. He did not write about insiders and outsiders – in his time only the academic outsider did research – but thanks to Malinowski, the study of culture moved from "objective" description to "participant observation."

Malinowski's interest in studying culture probably began at home. His father was a university professor who studied Polish dialect and folklore. As a young man, Bronislaw read Sir James Frazer's *The Golden Bough*, a classic tome on practices of religion and magic, and was fascinated by it. In university, he studied folk psychology, and, in 1910, he traveled to England to study at the London School of Economics, where the young field of anthropology had been formally established as a discipline.[1] He did doctoral and postdoctoral fieldwork in Papua New Guinea and then the Trobriand Islands, where, during the First World War, he spent an unprecedented amount of time, due to the political difficulties of travel during the war.[2]

During these extended field studies, he made breakthroughs that truly launched the field of cultural anthropology, writing vigorously on his insight that culture cannot be understood from the outside and cannot be captured meaningfully in brief descriptions sketched by "impartial," passive observers. He "broke with convention by abandoning the positivist pretense of aloof scientific objectivity by inserting a witnessing self into his narrative" (Young 2014, np). Malinowski famously taught that only through in-depth *participant observation* can the anthropologist fulfill the real work of anthropology: to grasp the native's point of view, *his* relation to life, to realize *his* vision, *his* world (*sic* in terms of the pronouns).

Malinowski was ahead of his time, but he was still a product of it. The language of the introduction to *Argonauts of the Pacific*, contrasting "native races" with "men of academic training," makes this quite clear:

> The research which has been done on native races by men of academic training has proved beyond doubt and cavil that scientific, methodic inquiry can give us results far more abundant and of better quality than those of even the best amateur's work. Most, though not all, of the modern scientific accounts have opened up quite new and unexpected aspects of tribal life. They have given us, in clear outline, the picture of social institutions often surprisingly vast and complex; they have brought before us the vision of the native as he is, in his religious and magical beliefs and practices. They have allowed us to penetrate into his mind far more deeply than we have ever done before.
>
> (Malinowski 1922, xi)

In a similar vein, Malinowski writes of "the hope of gaining a new vision of savage humanity through the labours of scientific specialists" (xi).

We will not "cancel" Malinowski for his use of such language ("savage humanity," etc.) or deride his male-centered, Euro-centered worldview. We are all products of our time, place and culture, including those of us writing and reading this book. Instead, we will appreciate his invaluable contribution that culture can only be truly understood from participants' lived experience and point of view and mark this as the beginning of our story.

The term "savage" began to fall away as a result of Malinowski's work. The understandings generated by participant observation showed that "native" cultures (a less loaded term than "savage") were every bit as sophisticated and complex as Western, European cultures. Before Malinowski, the westerner looking from the outside saw savages. Malinowski's contribution was to show us that when ethnographic work is conducted over time, through participant observations, complex human motivations and cultural rules and norms begin to be revealed. The researcher is still an outsider, but he or she is trying to understand the insider experience.

For the first seventy years or so of the twentieth century, it could be said that "[d]espite all of the diverse peoples, cultures, practices, and places that anthropologists have studied, the discipline has really operated with only one paradigm or model of ethnography, that of the traditions of Malinowski and Boas, refined over the past seventy years in several varieties of British and American anthropology" (Marcus 2002, 192).

During these years, there was development of the idea that culture could be viewed from the outside *and* from the inside, and new terminologies were introduced to the discussion.

In 1954, linguist Kenneth Pike coined the terms "emic" and "etic." These terms have come to be generally understood as insider (emic) and outsider (etic) knowledge, experience and perspectives. Pike took the terms from the linguistic terms "phonemic" and "phonetic." In linguistics, a phoneme is a particular set of sounds in a particular language, understandable by native speakers of that language. Phonetics is the study of speech sounds, across languages and in all languages. From here it is an easy leap to "emic" as "specific approaches to specific cultures" aimed at "eliciting within a particular culture that set of differences that make a difference. Conversely, 'etic' refers to general approaches resorting to universal or all-purpose analytical tools. Etic apprehends cultural systems in a comparative perspective" (Jorian 1983, 41).

Despite the refinement of these understandings that culture can be researched from the outside, through "objective" observation and description, as well as from the inside, through long-term, in-depth participant observation, and the generation of new terminology to help with this refinement of understanding, it took another philosophical, social and epistemological transition to move the discussion and practice of cultural study to a new plane.

We refer to the shift from modernism to postmodernism. Modernist ethnographic work remained based in its roots, "which have at times defined cultures, named people, and told them who they are and what they might become. In short, ethnography grew out of a master discourse on colonization" (Clair 2003, 3). Postmodernism is a complex topic of discussion, rife with heavy terminology and subject to endless definitions. We do not intend here to strew too much terminology or too many definitions on the path we are sketching. Suffice it to say, for our purposes (and this is a vast simplification), that postmodernist research rejects meta-narratives and "focuses on the problematic nature of representation" (Pool 1991, 315). Who has the right to write about whom? Who "knows" about a culture? Who can produce a "true" text?

Ethnographic reporting can today, since the "crises of representation and legitimization" that began in the 1980s (Denzin 1997), come in forms as diverse as drama, dance and art, but most research into culture still produces written text. Pool (1991, 326) argues that "ethnography is *necessarily* textual. Ethnographers transform cultures into texts, and these texts then become the objects of further anthropological study and theorizing. Textualized cultures are eternal, and can be analyzed and compared long after the 'real' cultures on which they were based have changed beyond recognition or disappeared completely." This is problematic, since today's ethnography is infused with phenomenology and is aimed at capturing *lived* experience. Like pinning a live butterfly to cardboard and then covering the lovely, dead thing with glass, writing culture captures a people and a time under glass. Paradoxically, this is also the great contribution of ethnography. Eternalizing culture not only preserves precious people and times but these written texts are also the sources from which we do try, from intimate details, to learn more about ourselves and others, and yes, to theorize, in order to learn and plan and work toward better human societies on the basis of knowledge about the multicolored human clan of which we are all a part.

So, if knowledge is to be captured, written and preserved in this way, what kind of research, and researchers, will produce ethnographic texts with high verisimilitude?[3] This brings us directly to insider-outsider research.

An important part of our discussion is researcher reflexivity, a term that emerged during the late 1970s to capture growing understanding that qualitative researchers must position themselves in relation to those they are researching; to ask, in effect, what comes from me, and what is really here. As Crick (1992, 175) put it, "The 'self' may be simultaneously enabling and disabling. . . . Since we cannot shed the self, we must give it a focal point in our writings." This raises issues of both validity (is what I think I have found here really true?) and ethics (am I imposing my worldview on these people, and thus betraying their trust?). Ethical issues arise in every kind of research. Since the 1960s, ethics in qualitative research has been an important topic of discussion (Guillemin and Gillam 2004), and this discussion is inextricably intertwined with researcher reflexivity, the ongoing researcher practice of self-inquiry. Court (2018, 11), drawing on Schon's conception of reflective practice (1987), says that reflective practice means

> ongoing personal inquiry into research processes, relations with the research population and emerging interpretations of data. *Reflectivity* is a personal propensity, discipline and practice by which a researcher inquires critically into his or her work. . . . *Reflexivity* is, by definition, two-directional, with cause and effect affecting one another. . . . When researchers reflect critically on their work they change the practice of research, which then conducts itself (as it were) differently. Reflexivity can be seen to be a broader term, a systematic inquiry into the entire context of knowledge construction through research.

In 1982, Jay Ruby published *A Crack in the Mirror*, an edited collection that has become a classic book on reflexivity. This book, a collection of essays by various anthropologists, explores what had already become by that time a central issue in qualitative research. The book expands on how reflexivity leads to cultural and methodological self-awareness.

So when do notions of insider and outsider research really enter this developing conversation? Insider and outsider positions are understood, if not exactly named, certainly at least from the time of the publication of *A Crack in the Mirror*. Adler and Adler (1987) talk about "membership roles": peripheral member researchers, who do not participate in the activities of the group being researched; active member researchers, who become involved with activities of the group being researched without adopting their lifestyles and values; and complete member researchers, who are part of the group being studied.

In a classic 1998 article, James Banks names four possible researcher positions in his typology of cross-cultural researchers: the Indigenous insider – a complete member of the group being researched; the Indigenous outsider – someone who was socialized in the group but has experienced high levels of socialization outside the group; the external insider – someone who was socialized in another culture but has adopted the values and behaviors of the group being researched; and the external outsider – someone who was socialized elsewhere and who has little understanding of the group being studied. We like this typology because it recognizes that "insider" and "outsider" are not absolute. According to Banks' typology, in the work we report in this book, Deborah is an external outsider, and Randa is somewhere between an Indigenous insider and an Indigenous outsider. Randa grew up in a Druze home, in a cloistered Druze village, and attended local Druze or mixed Muslim-Druze-Christian Arab schools. When she attended university and pursued advanced degrees, she became more and more socialized in academic culture. When we studied Druze schools, Deborah, though an outsider to Druze culture, was something like an external insider (though this doesn't quite work with Banks' definition): trained and experienced as a teacher and school principal, her knowledge of schools is rich and deep, even though she does not understand Arabic and is not of the religions practiced by the populations of these schools.

Terminology is less important than the development of the discourse. The discourse (still developing) for at least the last forty years has been, in effect, about epistemological privilege: Whose knowledge is privileged, whose knowledge is the most "true," what kinds of knowledge, from the "inside" or from the "outside," can produce analytic descriptions of cultures that have high verisimilitude. Are there any right answers to these questions? Flick (1998) sees insider-outsider positions as fluid, with even an outsider moving inward as he or she develops more and more knowledge about the culture under study. Flick names possible researcher positions as stranger, visitor, initiate and insider. These are not static, and they relate to the researcher's developing knowledge.

Ethical and methodological questions are infused in this discourse; ongoing examination of these questions means reflective practice by each researcher and reflexivity by the community of researchers. Reflexivity means that each research study and each researcher move the discourse forward.

We should note here that until perhaps the 1960s, ethnography generally referred to the study of a "foreign" culture, a culture that is far away, a culture in which the outsider really is from outside, in more ways than one. But ethnography, and qualitative research, in general, has for decades not been the purview only of anthropologists who study "foreign" cultures.

For one thing, "the other" lives in our neighborhood now, not across the ocean. In today's multicultural world, a rainbow of peoples and cultures live in the same city. "Urban anthropology," building on some ethnographic work as early as the 1930s and 1940s, became an established field in the 1960s, with early urban anthropologists studying urban poverty, persistent kinship patterns, residential neighborhood life, features of ethnicity, and so forth (Sanjek 1990). This was urban anthropology conducted by outsiders, people from the academic world, only a little less than were the early ethnographers studying "foreign" cultures.

In education, ethnographic study of classrooms and schools has been a major research approach since at least the 1970s, though its roots can be found in Margaret Mead's ethnographic work in Samoa, and "the convening of a conference by Margaret Mead in 1949, for the purpose of exploring the educational problems of special cultural groups, foreshadowed the direction of future educational ethnography and challenged notions of the detached observer" (Yon 2003, 413). Perhaps in educational ethnography more than in study of other areas, insider and outsider status was and is less fixed, less clear, because even the academic university researcher was once a student in school and quite often was a teacher before moving into academics.

Of course, it is legitimate for a single, outsider researcher or a team of outsider researchers to conduct a study, using participant observation and key informants to approach understanding of participants' lived experience. It is legitimate for a single, insider researcher to build on his or her insider connections, experience and insight and to make some research distance through extensive reflective work and references to literature. It is legitimate to assemble a mixed team of insiders and outsiders. All ethnographic work conducted rigorously, honestly and reflectively contributes to a greater understanding of ourselves and others and thus to creating a better world.

There is no "better" position for a researcher in relation to the research participants; there is always the need for researchers to reflect on their position, its benefits and drawbacks, and to act accordingly. We have spoken mostly in this chapter about outsider researchers, who are virtually always from the academic world. Research is an academic enterprise, for better or worse, though this enterprise has certainly moved toward becoming more egalitarian. What about insider researchers, then? Do they exist only partnered with an outsider researcher?

No; there are today many examples of insiders collecting life stories and oral histories with people from the culture in which the insider was raised[4] (e.g., Liu 2006, who documented Chinese women's life histories); very often in order to give voice to underrepresented, unheard persons and groups (e.g., Mitchell 2008, who interviewed nurses and patients with mental disabilities in the hospital where he was born, in the community where he grew up). The insider in these cases has become, according to Banks' insightful typology, an Indigenous outsider – someone who was socialized in the group but has experienced high levels of socialization outside the group – because academic researchers have taken a big step away from their Indigenous culture, absorbing the behaviors, knowledge and academic requirements of the academic world. This is Randa's position when she studies the Druze.

In a somewhat different context, organizational culture in the business world is often studied by insider researchers who are part of the workplaces they study, doing a kind of action research, conducting fieldwork in order to better understand their workplaces, to solve practical problems and to create new organizational knowledge (see Costley, Elliot and Gibbs 2010). In fact, participatory action research is always undertaken by insiders, with or without an outsider partnership. The literature is rife with the reports of teachers, nurses, factory workers, businesspersons and those from other professions, who conducted insider research in order to understand their own work and workplaces better and to make improvements.

Whether the culture under study is across the ocean or across the street, whether we live and work in the setting or are meeting it anew, we aim in this book to illustrate how an intimate pair, an "insider" and an "outsider" researcher, who are constantly and rigorously reflecting on their developing insights, their methods, their interpretations, can offer a powerful combination of viewpoints, insights and understandings, greater than the sum of its parts, forged through ongoing critical discussion, leading to research results with high verisimilitude. This process is rocky and exhilarating, the path strewn with dilemmas, the insights gained rich and deep.

Essential to any discussion of insider-outsider research is self-revelation on the part of the researchers. We thus move now to each of our stories.

Notes

1   As we said at the beginning of this chapter, there *was* anthropology before it was established as a discipline in 1908 at the London School of Economics. For readers interested in the story before Malinowski, the classic book by anthropologist George W. Stocking Jr., *Victorian Anthropology* (New York: MacMillan, 1982) is highly recommended. Regarding the use of the term "savage," Stocking tells us that "discussions of savages became institutionalized first as 'ethnology' and then as 'anthropology' between 1837 and 1871" (xii).

2   New World Encyclopedia (www.newworldencyclopedia.org/entry/Bronis%C5% 82aw_Malinowski).
Encyclopedia Britannica (www.britannica.com/biography/Bronislaw-Malinowski).

3   In *Conjectures and Refutations*, Karl Popper uses the term "verisimilitude" to mean "truthlikeness" as a way to evaluate the worth of a theory: "Ultimately, the idea of verisimilitude is most important in cases where we know that we have to work with theories which are at best approximations – that is to say, theories of which we know that they cannot be true. . . . In these cases we can still speak of better or worse approximations to the truth" (1963, 235). As qualitative research developed during the 1980s and beyond, verisimilitude came to mean "a text's . . . ability to reproduce (simulate) and map the real. Verisimilitude has been the most important criterion of traditional validity. It rests on the assumption that reality can be truthfully, faithfully and accurately captured" (Denzin 1997, 10).

4   See Melanie Greene 2014, "On the Inside Looking In: Methodological Insights and Challenges in Conducting Qualitative Insider Research" for a review of literature into insider research.

Chapter references

Adler, Patricia, and Peter Adler. 1987. *Membership Roles in Field Research*. Newbury Park, CA: Sage.

Banks, James A. 1998. "The Lives and Values of Researchers: Implications for Educating Citizens in a Multicultural Society." *Educational Researcher* 27 (4): 4–17. http://edr.sagepub.com/content/27/7/4.

Clair, Robin P. 2003. "An Overview of Ethnography." In *Expressions of Ethnography: Novel Approaches to Qualitative Methods*, edited by Robin Patric Clair, 3–28. Albany: State University of New York.

Costley, Carol, Geoffrey Elliot, and Paul Gibbs. 2010. *Doing Work-Based Research: Approaches to Enquiry for Insider Researchers*. Thousand Oaks, CA: Sage.

Court, Deborah. 2018. *Qualitative Research and Intercultural Understanding*. London and New York: Routledge.

Crick, Malcolm. 1992. "Ali and Me: An Essay on Street Corner Anthropology." In *Anthropology and Autobiography*, edited by J. Okely and H. Callaway. London: Routledge.

Denzin, Norman K. 1997. *Interpretive Ethnography: Ethnographic Practices for the 21st Century*. Thousand Oaks, CA: Sage.

Flick, Uwe. 1998. *An Introduction to Qualitative Research*. London: Sage.

Greene, Melanie. 2014. "On the Inside Looking in: Methodological Insights and Challenges in Conducting Qualitative Insider Research." *The Qualitative Report* 19 (29): 1–13. http://nsuworks.nova.edu/tqr/vol19/iss29/3.

Guillemin, Marilys, and Lynn Gillam. 2004. "Ethics, Reflexivity, and 'Ethically Important Moments' in Research." *Qualitative Inquiry* 10 (2): 261–80. https:// doi.org/10.1177%2F1077800403262360.

Hodgen, Margaret. 1964. *Early Anthropology in the Sixteenth and Seventeenth Centuries*. Philadelphia: University of Pennsylvania Press.

Jorian, Paul. 1983. "Emic and Etic: Two Anthropological Ways of Spilling Ink." *Cambridge Journal of Anthropology* 8 (3): 41–68. www.jstor.org/stable/23816293.

Levy-Zumwalt, Rosemary. 2019. *Franz Boas: The Emergence of the Anthropologist* (Critical Studies in the History of Anthropology). Nebraska: University of Nebraska Press.

Liu, Jieyu. 2006. "Researching Chinese Women's Lives: 'Insider' Research and Life History Interviewing." *Oral History* 34 (1): 43–52. www.jstor.org/stable/40179843.

Malinowski, Bronislaw. 1922. *Argonauts of the Western Pacific*. London: Routledge and Kegan Paul.

Marcus, George E. 2002. "Beyond Malinowski and After 'Writing Culture:' On the Future of Cultural Anthropology and the Predicament of Ethnography." *TAJA The Australian Journal of Anthropology* 13 (2): 191–99. https://doi.org/10.1111/j.1835-9310.2002.tb00199.x.

Mitchell, Howard. 2008. "The Insider Researcher." In *Understanding Health and Social Care: An Introductory Reader*, 2nd ed., edited by Julia Jonson and Corrine De Souza, 37–44. Thousand Oaks, CA and London: Sage.

Pool, Robert. 1991. "Postmodern Ethnography?" *Critique of Anthropology* 11 (4): 309–31. https://journals.sagepub.com/doi/pdf/10.1177/0308275X9101100402.

Popper, Karl. 1963. *Conjectures and Refutations: The Growth of Scientific Knowledge*. London: Routledge.

Ruby, Jay. 1982. *A Crack in the Mirror: Reflexive Perspectives in Anthropology*. Philadelphia, PA: University of Pennsylvania Press.

Sanjek, Roger. 1990. "Urban Anthropology in the 1980s: A World View." *Annual Review of Anthropology* 19: 151–86. https://doi.org/10.1146/annurev.an.19.100190.001055.

Schon, Donald. 1987. *The Reflective Practitioner*. New York: Basic Books.

Stocking, George. 1982. *Victorian Anthropology*. New York and Toronto: MacMillan.

Webster, Joan Parker, and Theresa Arevgaq John. 2010. "Preserving a Space for Cross-Cultural Collaborations: An Account of Insider/Outsider Issues." *Ethnography and Education* 5 (2): 175–91. https://doi.org/10.1080/17457823.2010.493404.

Yon, Daniel A. 2003. "Highlights and Overview of the History of Educational Ethnography." *Annual Review of Anthropology* 32: 411–29. https://doi.org/10.1146/annurev.anthro.32.061002.093449.

Young, Michael W. 2014. "Writing His Life Through the Other: The Anthropology of Malinowski." *The Public Domain Review*, January. https://publicdomainreview.org/essay/writing-his-life-through-the-other-the-anthropology-of-malinowski.

2   Our stories

On the many shades of insider and outsider status

One of the things that became very clear as we began to reflect on and write about our research relationship is that shades of insider and outsider status are subtle and multifaceted. Yes, in our collaborative studies into Israeli Druze culture, Randa is the insider and Deborah the outsider; no question about it. But many other contexts come into play, other cultures to which each of us has affiliation and various levels of knowledge and experience. School culture, academic culture, family culture and Israeli culture – all of these are parts of our backgrounds in various ways, and our experiences in these contexts affect our interpretations and insights. While we will continue to speak of Randa as the insider and Deborah as the outsider in our research into the Israeli Druze, the shades of positioning, status and familiarity are more finely drawn than we have ever seen presented in the literature. It is through that which is familiar that we find our way into understanding that which is new. This is, in effect, essential – how can we name and begin to comprehend something we have never known, seen or imagined? – but it is also fraught with danger. It is too easy to stay with the familiar names and categories that allowed our entry into understanding. Will we be able to free ourselves from those helpful fetters and truly see that which is new, that which is beyond our own experience? This is the outsider's challenge. And, conversely, it is seeing familiar things with new eyes that enables us to shed new light on them. Cultural elements that are part of us need to be taken out of their comfortable inner place and named, then examined and asked, why? This is the insider's challenge.

There is much to be said for the well-known, almost cliched phrase, "making the strange familiar and the familiar strange."[1] Who among us did not learn in cultural anthropology and qualitative research courses that we must as researchers learn to do this? This notion is key to insider-outsider research. Though its origins are murky, the phrase is often attributed to the

DOI: 10.4324/9781003268628-3

eighteenth-century German poet Novalis, who applied it to the work of the artist, whose task, he said, is to help us see familiar things in a new light, to see mysterious and beautiful qualities to which familiarity has blinded us, as well as to recognize familiar qualities in things that seem strange. The idea was taken up by sociology and anthropology and remains an insightful encapsulation of our challenge as qualitative researchers. This great challenge can be, in our experience, effectively tackled by an intimate pair of researchers who come with different biographies, different sets of knowledge, and who can work intensively and honestly, to argue, listen, revisit and reframe, until an analysis of high verisimilitude is reached.

Randa, in her own words

Early on in our relationship, I was interviewed by my friend Deborah. Among the things I told her, I said,[2]

> From the time I was little, I did not accept my parents. All the time I said, "You are not my parents." I got angry at my parents that they took me from other parents. And this was so extreme that I was unhealthy. The doctors did not even give my parents much hope that I would live. My mother always gave me medicines and vitamins to get stronger, because I was weak and very thin. I always looked for a place to be alone, I was closed within myself. Why? I said to my mother, "You are not my mother, I don't live in a small village, I live in a large town, with only brothers."

My father understood what was happening with his young daughter.

> Not everyone remembers, but everyone knows it's possible that someone might remember his or her former life, and everyone gets it right away. My father understood me. I also had an old grandfather who in the past had worked with the Turks, and when I was little I said words in Turkish. When he came to visit he heard me and said, "She is speaking Turkish and not Arabic!"

My people, the Druze, believe in reincarnation. A very few people remember a previous incarnation. I did. I had been a young woman killed by accident in my home in Turkey while playing with my brother. Perhaps because of this memory, from the beginning I was different.

The Druze are a closed community of souls, souls that return in an endless cycle to new Druze bodies. We are a community of people with no land of our own, who have survived through the centuries through fierce loyalty to family and clan, and through unwavering adherence to tradition, including prohibition of marrying a non-Druze, remaining celibate until marriage, and showing great respect to parents and elders. Our religion is secret, its inner depths known only to religious Druze, those who strictly adhere to all the rules laid down by the sheikhs. For women, this means not leaving the village unless accompanied by a first-degree male relative, always wearing modest, traditional dress and not mingling in mixed company, among other things. A woman may not drive. These prohibitions effectively prevent her from pursuing higher education. Nowadays, more and more girls do pursue higher education, get driving licenses and work in mixed settings, and these women cannot be formally religious, they cannot be admitted to the inner secrets, though they continue to follow Druze values of respect for parents, family and community, dressing modestly and marrying only within the Druze community. These young women's fathers and husbands who support their choices may also be subject to religious strictures and excluded from the inner religious circle.

Perhaps because I remembered my previous incarnation, I was always older than my years, ambitious, eager for knowledge and accomplishment. My father, despite community norms, supported and encouraged me.

It has always been a struggle to be a good Druze woman and an academic career woman at the same time. In so many ways, these are opposing sets of values. As I began to advance academically, I felt pulled in two directions, with my community both admiring me, leaders showing me off to demonstrate how progressive they are, and criticizing me, subjecting me to various social slights and exclusions. Soon after I finished my doctorate (one of the very first Druze women to do so), this occurred.

I will never forget this, Sheik –, the spiritual leader of the Druze, called me at home and invited me to a meeting with the rector of (a large Israeli) University. I said okay, and I didn't know what to think, I thought I was in a dream, not in reality. I hung up the telephone and my husband said, "Who was it?" I said, "It was Sheik –. He invited me to a meeting with the rector of – University tomorrow." I immediately called the political leader of our community, and he said, "Don't worry, Randa, we will also invite another woman, you won't be the only one, and you two will represent the women of our community." I considered not going to the meeting. I didn't want to be another ornament. On the other hand, I do want to be inside. That's been the story all along, and I'm always wrestling with it. Do they respect me or am I just for show? I'm really burned out with this. I had these thoughts, for and against. . . . On the one hand I want to part of the Druze community and represent the women, and change their standing a bit, and on the other hand, there is a chance that these things will obstruct me in my own personal development. Is it really worthwhile for me, or not? All the time that I was studying, driving, making my own decisions, they criticized me, but I persevered. Now, all the time I am "in public." People want to use me, and at the same time they criticize me because I don't stay home with my husband and children.

Can I be all these things? Can I be a respectable Druze woman who loves her community and respects its values, a wife and mother, a researcher, a seeker of advanced academic degrees, a change agent for women, a social activist, an educational leader, the first woman from Israeli Arab and Druze society to serve as head of an academic college? For my Jewish-sector friends or those who are somewhere in the United States or Europe, this career path is something normal, natural and understandable. It is not special and unusual.

For women from Arab, Druze society, or for a woman who is a member of a minority group or a traditional society, it *is* a special and unusual thing, a phenomenon unusual in its dimensions. Women who did not grow up in a traditional society or as members of a minority cannot understand the determination and strength of action required to follow this path. They can never understand the social difficulties, the traditional codes that must be broken, the expectations of society from the role and place of the woman within traditional society that must be overcome. Therefore, from the experience of my friends who do not come from traditional or minority backgrounds, my success is a regular kind of success. But for my friends from minorities or traditional societies, mine is a remarkable success story. I will elaborate on the cases and phenomena that spring from my background as this book unfolds. For now, the important thing to note is that my starting point as an internal researcher is completely different from the point of origin of a researcher who belongs to another sector in Israel.

That is, being an integral part of a society influences our perception of the phenomenon or the event – being an integral part of a society as secretive and little-understood as the Druze compounds the complexity. This raises the question of the research contribution from the analysis of a phenomenon or case by two researchers from two different worlds.

Meeting Deborah was a pivotal point in my development. Being able to study my community and thus to understand it so much better, being able to publish academic articles so that the world can know who we are, can understand us, being able to use my academic knowledge for the good of my community, being a success story who serves as an example and model for those young women struggling as I did – these are some of the fruits of our research partnership.

Deborah, in her own words

In early middle age, I interrupted my academic career and moved with my husband to Israel to be close to family and to Jewish history and tradition. I did not know Hebrew. After studying in an *ulpan* (intensive Hebrew language class) for six months, I started teaching at a university; teaching, I must add, in atrocious Hebrew. I often did not understand what students said in response to my painstakingly prepared lessons. Israel is a cornucopia of cultural groups, and Hebrew is spoken in a stunning array of accents: mainstream "Israeli" Ashkenazi Hebrew, Sephardic Hebrew with different vowel sounds, Hebrew spoken by native Arabic speakers, Hebrew spoken by native speakers of English, Russian, Spanish, French, Amharic and more. People use Hebrew slang that does not appear in any dictionary. Understanding all these accents, combined with slang, grammatical constructions and all the vocabulary that I simply hadn't learned yet, was a kind of intellectual and cultural overload that required constant vigilance, learning and patience. I was an insider to academic culture and Jewish culture, but to Israeli culture, an outsider. From huge, polite Canada to tiny, hot, hot-blooded Israel – this was a change of huge proportions. As well as the language, small, daily events, manner of speaking and behaviors, like standing politely in line (Israelis generally do not), to the enthusiastic Israeli driving style, which involves a lot of tailgating and lurching from lane to lane without signaling – because of all these things, it took me years to begin to feel at home. I was used to being part of the mainstream and never questioning my place in it. The experience of outsiderness in Israel has been part of much of my academic writing since I arrived in Israel. And I have to say, it has been good for me. As a comfortable, mainstream Canadian comfortably researching Canadian schools, I never experienced meaningful outsiderness.

Even in Canada, as a qualitative researcher, I strived to position myself in relation to research participants but have done so much more since I began doing research in Israel. Among the early attempts was a 2006 article[3] written after a study of the mixed Muslim, Christian and Druze school in which Randa was teaching. She acted as my translator and research assistant while completing her master's degree and still teaching. In the preface to this article, I wrote:

> The proverbial stranger in a strange land, I arrived at the middle school in an Israeli Arab community in order to see in action a school I had been told exemplified positive values of peaceful co-existence. A Canadian immigrant to Israel, I neither speak Arabic nor have the kind of visceral knowledge of the Israeli school system that I do of the Canadian

system. I know Canadian education in my bones, having participated in it as a student, teacher, principal and teacher educator for forty years. While much is familiar in almost any school anywhere, the culture of Jewish Israeli schools still holds for me a subtle strangeness. An Arab Israeli school has the added dimensions of language and religion that I do not share. As in all the research I have done since I came to Israel, I struggled to make visible, to those at the school and especially to myself, the ways in which my own background as a Canadian, an English speaker, a grandmother, a Jew – all the myriad experiences that make me who I am – might influence my perceptions and understandings. For instance, since the birth of my grandchildren, my hope that terrorism and violence will end has become passionately intertwined with my fervent hope that, together with all the children, they will have long and peaceful lives. The profound change from huge, tranquil Canada to tiny, strife-ridden Israel has sensitized me to the notion of culture, to the subtleties of a researcher's insider or outsider status, and to the complexity of the quest for objectivity in ethnographic research. The very richness of such work comes from the researcher's data-based but always subjective delving into the subjective experiences of others.

Oddly, then, though I came to Israel from a university culture, my status as a researcher in Israel is always, even today, that of an outsider. Yes, a complete outsider to Druze culture but an outsider also in Israel. Somewhat paradoxically, Randa, who is part of the Arab minority but is a native-born Israeli, is in most ways more Israeli than I will ever be.

We do not wish to get lost here in the shades of insider and outsider status that come to light from our stories, but it is important to stress again that researcher status is not as clear-cut as it might at first glance appear to be.

Meeting Randa was a pivotal point in my development. I felt an immediate affinity with her and was inspired from the beginning by her intelligence and fierce determination. I have learned so very much through our association, not only about the Druze but also about culture, about method, about the profoundly human enterprise of qualitative research itself and about the search for elusive, imperfect truths that translate into academic articles. I have understood in a mature way that publishing academic articles is not just about the necessary business of academic advancement. Research sheds new light in order to make things better in some way for people and communities. Randa and I hope that our collaborative work has helped readers to know something of the beauty and wisdom of the Druze people and to help Druze women find their place in the modern world without damaging the community values from which they spring. We hope that in some small ways, our work sheds light on the possibilities for peaceful coexistence in a world of strife. There is no question that whatever contributions each of us has made are greater because of our collaboration.

We move in the next chapters to examination of vignettes from studies we conducted, highlighting the dilemmas, roadblocks and conundrums that arose in each, the insights, solutions and learnings at which we arrived, in order to shed some new light on insider-outsider research. Some of the concepts we will encounter along the way are cultural codes, trust, epistemic responsibility, researcher instinct, standpoint theory, positionality, intersectionality, identity politics, rapport, time and voice and more. In the final chapter, we will attempt to tie it all together in order to offer, as promised by the title of this book, new insights on method and meaning in insider-outsider research.

Notes

1 See Myers "The Familiar Strange and the Strange Familiar in Anthropology and Beyond," 2011, for an excellent historical tracing of the use of this phrase in anthropology.
2 The quotations used in this chapter are taken from our article, "The View from the Bridge," 2011.
3 This quote, slightly shortened, is from "Foolish Dreams in a Fabled Land," Deborah Court, 2006.

Chapter references

Court, Deborah. 2006. "Foolish Dreams in a Fabled Land: Living Coexistence in an Israeli Middle School." *Curriculum Inquiry* 36 (2): 189–208. https://doi.org/10.1111/j.1467-873X.2006.00352.x.
Court, Deborah, and Randa Abbas. 2011. "The View from the Bridge: An Israeli Druze Woman as Guardian of Religious Tradition and Agent of Social Change." *The International Journal of Religion and Spirituality in Society* 1 (1): 135–46. https://doi.org/10.18848/2154-8633/CGP/v01i01/50990.
Myers, Robert. 2011. "The Familiar Strange and the Strange Familiar in Anthropology and Beyond." *General Anthropology* 18 (2): 1, 7–9. https://anthrosource.onlinelibrary.wiley.com/doi/epdf/10.1111/j.1939-3466.2011.00007.x?saml_referrer.

3 Unearthing cultural codes
A visit to the graveyard

Cultural codes and the roles of the insider and outsider

As we began to speak about writing this book, one of the questions that Deborah asked Randa over and over was, "But what is *my* role? The insider knowledge is yours. I would never have been admitted to those homes, those schools, or if I had been, I would not have been told the things that you were told. And if I had been told those things, I would not have understood them in the way that you did. Yes, when we began, I came with knowledge of academic publishing, of research methods, and of the English language, of which you were not yet fully possessed, but those are *technical* aspects of our work. What did I contribute in terms of insight into Druze culture?" The bigger question was (and is), why is it not simply better for insiders to study their own cultures? They have access, they have the trust of participants and they have their own lived experience of the culture. Who needs an outsider?

Deborah came to the conclusion that, put in the simplest form possible, the outsider's role is to ask *why*: to be alert and to look with interest at behaviors and traditions that are unquestioned by the participants themselves, asking Randa, why do they do this? Why don't they do that?

Randa had more to say on the topic! "Well, here's one thing. In an overall way, our relationship has helped me, the insider, wear the hat of the outsider, to deal with the whole Israeli society. Having really looked for the first time at my own culture's codes, I have learned better how to understand others' codes – Muslim, Christian, Jewish – and to know how to speak in different settings – and also when not to speak. And together we bring an important message to the world about the Druze! You strengthened me – you helped me be the bridge that I have become."

This is a fascinating notion that one role of the outsider is to help the insider build a bridge – or better yet, *become* a bridge – from his or her lived experience to the outside world, excavating tacit knowledge and making it explicit and then translating it into new vocabulary so that it can be shared. This, in

DOI: 10.4324/9781003268628-4

a nutshell, is the work of the insider-outsider partnership. And much of this excavation of tacit insider knowledge means identifying cultural codes.

Before looking at codes, let us take a step back and ask, what is culture? We use the term in many contexts – school culture, business culture – but what does it mean to talk about the culture of a group of people? In a formulation that remains unparalleled, Geertz (1973, 89) described culture as "an historically transmitted pattern of meanings embodied in symbols, a system of inherited conceptions expressed in symbolic form by means of which men [sic] communicate, perpetuate and develop their knowledge about and attitudes towards life." This "historically transmitted pattern of meanings" is contained in what most social scientists call cultural codes.

First of all, what is a code? A straightforward dictionary definition tells us that a code is a system of words, letters, figures or symbols used to represent others, especially for the purposes of secrecy. Codes are used by the military to confuse the enemy when messages are transmitted. Computer codes are special languages used to create computer programs, to tell the computer what to do. In each of these cases, meanings are contained in languages or symbols that do not overtly state those meanings; the meanings are known only to the people who know the code.

We also talk about moral and ethical codes that provide guidelines for behavior. In a classic book in which he attempts to unpack the ethics of the Navajo people, Ladd (1957) defines what he calls *normative ethics*, what are usually called practical ethics, as centering on questions like, what should I do? What is right, and what is wrong? What does it mean to live a good life? How should I live? When a person, group or community agrees on answers to these questions, this means they agree to live by these answers and counsel others to do so as well. Ladd differentiates between normative ethics and *descriptive ethics*, which ask for a description of people's answers to these questions. You think that is right? You think people should live this way? Why? Descriptive ethics ask for explanation, rationalization and opinion; they are one or two steps removed from actual conduct. Ladd argues that studying the descriptive ethics of cultures other than our own can "suggest new ways of approaching and solving moral problems . . . it may help us become more aware of our own presuppositions about ethics, and thus make us more critical of our own approach to ethical problems" (Ladd 1957, 2).

Ladd's analysis provides a partial answer to the perennial question of why we do research at all. Humans are curious and love to learn. It seems to us that these basic human elements, curiosity and love of learning, are directed toward enriching our own lives and the lives of others through acquiring new knowledge and gaining insight into different ways of doing and being.

Metaphorically parallel to the way computer codes contain messages and commands, cultural codes contain messages and commands for how a group of people should live their lives. These messages and commands are embedded in a web of values and beliefs about right and wrong and about the nature of the good life. They are also strongly connected with emotions. We learn the codes of our culture as children, through our experiences of love, happiness, belonging and adult censure or anger when we break rules, and these feelings imprint upon us the norms and rules of our culture (Rapaille 2006). This emotion-laden learning inspires in us loyalty to and love of, or at the very least, comfort with, our own culture. Think about it. You, dear reader, may be British, American, German, Japanese and so forth, and whatever criticisms you may have of your own country and culture, that culture is the deepest part of you. In our work, Deborah was continually moved by the love of the Druze people, including Randa, for their culture, despite their criticisms of some of the laws and rules. Deborah, an Israeli citizen for more than twenty-five years, remains deeply Canadian and feels a comfort level she feels nowhere else when she returns to Canada. Randa moves in international academic circles now, but she is at home in a Druze town, a Druze home, in a deep and simple way that she experiences nowhere else. The connection between learning and emotion has been well documented (Hascher 2010); learning one's native culture creates an emotion-laden self on which cultural codes are imprinted.

Studying culture always means identifying and unpacking cultural codes, codes that may on first glance obscure meaning but that are rich with meaning for those who learn and live them.

Cultural codes are those symbols and systems of meaning that have a specific relevance to members of a particular group or society (Hyatt and Simons 1999, 24).

> Codes . . . control both the creation and organization of specific meanings and the conditions for their transmission and reception. At the same time, code and codification concern translation: the transcription and transition of information between social or experiential domains or levels, contexts or situations. Does information remain the same through the translation process? Is it even possible to "translate" between different perceptions, different generalities, different societies and cultures?
>
> (Rapport 2014, 57)

These are troubling questions. Does our work together, and Randa's work as a bridge, capture truths about the Druze? Or, even though she lives in this culture, are meanings lost in translation? What happens when tacit cultural codes are revealed to the insider, who holds them up to the light and examines them, as it were, for the first time? What happens when she translates them for the outsider?

As we discussed these questions in preparation for writing this book, Randa gave an example. "You don't go into a graveyard," she said. "You just don't. To me this has always been obvious, not something that needed to be discussed or asked about. My mother and father are both dead, and I have never visited their graves. Only when you said – what? Why not? – did I understand that this is not normal among other people. Only when you asked *why* did I begin to unpack the many layers of this unquestioned rule."

A visit to the graveyard

One of the foundational beliefs of the Druze religion is that Druze souls are continually reborn into new Druze bodies. At the moment of death, or shortly after a Druze person dies, his or her soul migrates to the body of a Druze baby that is about to be born (Abu Azaldin 1990). For this reason, there may be no intermarriage. The Druze are a closed community of souls. No one can convert or decide to be Druze; Druze are born and die as Druze, and they marry only within their own community. The belief in reincarnation is one of the pillars that protect the Druze, who are a minority wherever they live, against assimilation and the loss of their communal self that would surely follow.

The Druze religion is an offshoot of Islam, splitting away in Egypt in the tenth century CE. The Druze do not follow the five pillars of Islam, they do not pray five times a day toward Mecca and, unlike the Muslims, Druze men may marry only one wife.[1] The Druze do not have and have never had a country of their own. Most Druze live in the Middle East, mainly in Syria, Israel, Lebanon and Jordan, but during the nineteenth and early twentieth centuries, small immigrant communities were established in Canada, Australia, the United States, parts of Europe and parts of South and Central America. The secrecy of the religion, the strong family and community values and the absolute centrality of reincarnation have sustained them through the centuries, against discrimination, persecution and assimilation.

The Druze have no country of their own and are fiercely loyal to the country in which they reside, always maintaining good relations with the government and the mainstream local population. In Israel, Druze men are the only group other than Jews who serve mandatory service in the army, the Israeli Defense Forces (IDF). They serve loyally, bravely and proudly, with many men making a career in the army after their mandatory service. Many Druze soldiers have fought alongside their Jewish countrymen, and no small number have died.

Israel, surrounded on all sides by hostile neighbors, has fought several wars for its survival, and one of the saddest days of the year is Remembrance Day for Fallen Soldiers (*yom hazikaron* – Remembrance Day). On this day Jewish families (as well as the smaller number of Bedouin and Christian families whose sons chose to serve and died) visit the graves of their fallen sons and daughters (Jewish women may serve in the army), sisters and brothers, husbands and wives, mothers and fathers. Many Israelis who have not lost someone also visit military cemeteries on this day to pay their respects and to remember that, as in every country, it is the strong, brave young who protect the country and sometimes make the ultimate sacrifice.

Because the Druze believe absolutely in reincarnation, they do not, after burying a loved one, ever visit the cemetery again. The soul is not there with the body; the soul has moved on to a new body, a new Druze life. The Druze do not visit their cemeteries because it is forbidden; continuing to mourn in the place of a buried body belies the absolute belief that the person has moved on.

But in Israel, where Druze men (not women) fight and die in the army, the sheikhs, the religious leaders who set religious policy and enforce the policy and rules that surround the core Druze beliefs, have made a remarkable exception. On Remembrance Day for Fallen Soldiers, and only on this day, the Druze may visit the graves of their dead in military cemeteries. It is difficult to explain the magnitude of this religious concession and the meanings embedded in it. These meanings came into relief for Randa only when we discussed this together, and she began to explain it to Deborah.

One of Randa's studies involved an investigation into how Druze high schools work to strengthen both students' Druze identity *and* their Israeli identity and sense of citizenship (Abbas 2020). This is no small challenge for a school, its teachers, leaders and curriculum designers. The Druze are part of Israel's Arabic-speaking population, and because of the affinity created through shared language, there are of course central Arab aspects of their identity, which includes identification with the Palestinians as much as with the multicultural but declaredly Jewish state of Israel. Language is a strong connector between people. Fishman (2010, xxiii) actually says that languages are "societally linked human codes," holding within them attitudes, values and behaviors, not merely vocabulary and grammar. The literature in a particular language, its stories, heroes and myths become part of the consciousness of people who hear and read this literature from childhood. Much of culture is contained in language.

The Israeli Druze, who are Arab but not Muslim or Christian, are, like the Druze wherever they live, an island, albeit a complex one. They are Arabic-speaking Arabs, linked to other Arabs by shared language and culture;

they are their own unique Druze selves, linked to each other because of their shared, reclusive history and secretive religion, and they are also loyal citizens of their homeland, fulfilling all their roles as active citizens. These different identity components may combine in harmony, and they may also cause identity conflicts. Such "social identity complexity" is defined as "perceived overlap in membership across pairs of ingroups, with lower overlap reflecting higher complexity" (Miller, Brewer, and Arbuckle 2009, 79). The Druze, perhaps especially the young, certainly have overlap between their Arab, Druze and Israeli identity components.[2] Each of the aspects of Druze identity is valuable and should be nurtured. Arabic language and literature are strengthened in school. Druze identity is strengthened at home and in the local community. Israeli identity is strengthened, at least in large part, by service, and often lifelong careers, in the IDF.

Randa and Deborah went together to interview one of the Druze high school principals during Randa's school study, and the topic of taking students to visit the Druze military cemetery on Remembrance Day was raised. The principal spoke of how important these visits are to the work of the school in strengthening Israeli identity. This conversation with the principal, and our conversation afterward, caused Deborah to ask questions and caused Randa to really look, for the first time, at the significance of these Remembrance Day cemetery visits.

The making of this religious concession by the sheikhs – to allow visits on Remembrance Day to the graves of soldiers who died in the army – is almost without precedent. That the sheikhs now allow visits to Druze military cemeteries, completely contrary to the Druze practice and belief against visiting graves, speaks of the great loyalty of the Druze to the country in which they live. The sheikhs themselves, in making this ruling, had to find a difficult balance between their deepest religious beliefs and national loyalty. High schools hold these ceremonies as part of strengthening the Israeli aspect of Druze students' identities, and villagers come to the military cemeteries on Remembrance Day to lay flowers and show their respect to fallen soldiers and thus to the state. This is in direct conflict with the centuries-old religion stricture against visiting cemeteries, a stricture laid down because of the absolute belief in reincarnation. This cannot be stressed enough.

What would seem in other cultures to be a fairly simple and obvious act – individuals and whole communities visiting military cemeteries on Remembrance Day to honor the soldiers in their village who died fighting in the army – is revealed to be imbued with great meaning. That the sheikhs, whose role is to guard the Druze religion against the onslaught of change in modern times, would make this concession shows how importantly they view Druze national loyalty, exemplified by service in the IDF.

These meanings were revealed to both of us through intense and ongoing discussion, the kind of discussion that has developed over the years of our work together. We stated at the beginning of this book that a research *partnership* is qualitatively different than a shorter-term research *team* – a group of outsiders who assemble with insiders/key informants for a specific project in order to see a culture from within and without. Such teamwork is important work, and we most certainly do not intend to denigrate it. We wish to suggest that for those who intend to engage in long-term study of a particular cultural group, the development of long-term insider-outsider research relationships is highly recommended. Our relationship was perhaps serendipity in its beginning, but its development over the years has led us to a profound level of *trust* in one another and to our self-definition as *partners*.

How does trust enter into the research story? Deborah's role as an outsider is to look, to see and to ask why, to not be afraid to ask, despite her deep Canadian politeness, trusting that Randa will not be offended, will take the question seriously and will open herself up to what may become a rather personal discussion. "Why," after all, asks about Randa's own life, culture, beliefs, values and feelings. Randa's role as an insider is to look with new eyes at the known, the taken-for-granted, and to trust that Deborah's listening and probing will be respectful, patient and appreciative. Without this deep trust on both sides, cultural codes will not be identified, unpacked, translated and their meanings brought to light. One of the things Deborah has learned through this partnership is how Randa's "becoming a bridge" – telling the world about her culture – is a burning light inside her, pushing her into further research. She *loves* her people. If the Druze are an island, then Randa is a bridge that joins that island to other islands; to growth, insight and communication while nevertheless protecting her culture. This is a further challenge of the insider: What to reveal? What should remain private? What to protect? We examine this in the next chapter.

Notes

1 See www.britannica.com/topic/Druze for more details about Druze beliefs and history.
2 See Abbas and Court 2021, chapter two, for a thorough discussion of identity among younger Israeli Druze.

Chapter references

Abbas, Randa Khair. 2020. "How Do School-Based Ceremonies Contribute to Adolescents' Identity Design? A Case Study in Two Druze High Schools." *Citizenship Teaching and Learning* 15 (3): 323–40. https://doi.org/10.1386/ctl_00037_1.

Abbas, Randa Khair, and Deborah Court. 2021. *The Israeli Druze Community in Transition: Between Tradition and Modernity.* Newcastle Upon Tyne, UK: Cambridge Scholars Publishing.

Abu Azaldin, Najla. 1990. *The Druze in History.* Beirut: Dar Al Alam Lalmalain. Arabic.

Fishman, Joshua. 2010. "Sociolinguistics: Language and Ethnic Identity in Context." In *Handbook of Language and Ethnic Identity*, 2nd ed., edited by Joshua Fishman and Ofelia Garcia, xxiii–xxxv. Oxford: Oxford University Press.

Geertz, Clifford. 1973. *The Interpretation of Cultures.* New York: Basic Books.

Hascher, Tina. 2010. "Learning and Emotion: Perspectives for Theory and Research." *European Educational Research Journal* 9 (1): 13–28. https://doi.org /10.2304%2Feerj.2010.9.1.13.

Hyatt, Jenny, and Helen Simons. 1999. "Culture Codes – Who Holds the Key?" *Evaluation* 5 (1): 23–41. https://doi.org/10.1177%2F13563899922208805.

Ladd, John. 1957. *The Structure of a Moral Code: Navajo Ethics.* Harvard: Harvard University Press.

Miller, Kevin, Marilynn Brewer, and Nathan Arbuckle. 2009. "Social Identity Complexity: Its Correlates and Antecedents." *Group Processes and Intergroup Relations* 12 (1): 79–94. https://doi.org/10.1177%2F1368430208098778.

Rapaille, Clotaire. 2006. *The Culture Code: An Ingenious Way to Understand Why People Around the World Buy and Live the Way They Do.* New York: Crown Publishing Group.

Rapport, Nigel. 2014. *Social and Cultural Anthropology: The Key Concepts.* 3rd ed. London and New York: Routledge.

4 All in the family

Unraveling the strands of a crowded interview

On epistemic responsibility

We will not engage here in the long-standing discussion of whether knowledge is in important ways subjective (it is: knowledge requires a knower), nor will we go to postmodernist extremes and claim that knowledge is absolutely subjective; such a claim makes a mockery of the search for truth in qualitative research. The practice of research assumes that there are truths to be discovered.

Because, as mundane as it may sound, we do seek truth: the truth (as Malinowski told us) of research participants – *their* lived experience, *their* meanings, the ways in which *they* understand their worlds. We earnestly seek these local truths in order to approach better understanding of the human condition, the myriad ways we live our lives, the qualities and practices that connect us, and, through understanding, to find ways to make things better. Research into different communities, and the understandings that research produces, can provide antidotes to racism and prejudice and mark the path forward toward celebrating our multicolored human garden.

We can, of course, never achieve a complete understanding of others' lives, but responsible researchers use all the tools at their disposal to reasonably approach the goal. The truth-seeking toolkit, if such a crude analogy can be applied, includes multiple data collection sources and extensive time in the field, as well as the human elements of listening, empathy, self-reflection, patience and careful reading not only of the lines but also between them. As we argue in this book, when it is possible, the close collaboration of an insider with an outsider researcher can contribute to the discovery of "true knowledge." The research enterprise is a huge responsibility. The danger of misunderstanding and misrepresenting others always looms.

Knowledge seeking, as Lorraine Code tells us, is "a cooperative-collaborative, textured human practice. . . . Thinking how knowers might achieve such a goal is an ongoing project in social epistemology, as is evaluating

DOI: 10.4324/9781003268628-5

epistemic responsibility in its fundamental connections with trust" (Code 2020, xi, xvii–xviii). What does it mean to be epistemically responsible? This is a heady philosophical topic, but in the context of qualitative research, it can be reasonably concentrated to these elements: Epistemic responsibility is fundamentally a *normative concept* (Bonjour 1985); it can be renamed as *epistemic trustworthiness* (Lehrer 2000): It involves and requires trust between participants and researchers, in order to produce knowledge that can be trusted; it involves an epistemic agent earnestly seeking justified reasons to believe that something is true (Corlett 2008). This process of earnest truth-seeking can be called *epistemic vigilance* (Origgi 2010).

We like the concept of responsibility in qualitative research. Researchers are responsible to themselves, their craft and, most important, their participants, to discover and communicate true knowledge. Discovery takes place during data collection and analysis. Communication means translating words, feelings and observations and condensing a sea of data into an article, book or research report, selecting, interspersing interpretations with raw data, sometimes leaping across languages, all the while trying to hold fast to the shining light of elusive, imperfect truth: This is epistemic responsibility in qualitative research.

Trust is key. Readers of research reports, although they may read with a critical eye, should be able to feel they are reading trustworthy results, based on work that was carried out responsibly. In terms of our work together, Randa as the insider has the trust of research participants, and she feels great responsibility to be an honest messenger for her community. Deborah as the outsider contributes a kind of objectivity that is important in translating our findings into academic format. The trust between us has been central to our ability to discover, interpret and communicate knowledge about the Druze community.

All in the family

One of the largest studies we conducted together (whose results were reported fully in Abbas and Court 2021) was commissioned and funded by the Israeli Ministry of Education in 2011. The topic was the generation gap – in perceptions of their community, personal identity, future aspirations, values and levels of religiosity – between Druze Israelis in their late teens and early 20s and those of their parents' generation, people in their 40s–60s. We did end up stretching these age boundaries to some extent, as in the interview discussed later.[1] For this study we conducted a total of sixty in-depth, semi-structured interviews with people of the younger and older generations. All of the interviews were conducted in people's homes.

For Deborah, simply driving from Druze village to Druze village was an education. The Israeli Druze live mostly in the north of the country, in mountain villages in the Galilee hills. Randa knows the villages, and she drove us from place to place over the space of several months. She arranged all the interviews, through personal connections of one kind or another. We were welcomed to every house and were often served a full meal before the interview. We brought a present to some homes, and Randa always knew when this was appropriate. The homes are beautifully decorated with rugs, ornate furniture, books and pictures of Druze sheikhs and saints.

On one dark, foggy evening, we drove a twisty, winding road up to a village where we were to interview both a woman we called Yasmin, a stay-at-home mother, and her husband, a businessman and politician. The husband never made it home that evening, supposedly because of the fog, although Randa said later that she thought this was his way out of being interviewed. Her instinct was that he had agreed to the interview in order to be polite but that he, as a well-known Druze politician, did not want to talk in front of his very traditional, religious, village-bound wife about the parties and social activities in which he participates and from which she is excluded. This was Randa's insider instinct based in knowledge of the chemistry in families where the wife is religious and the husband is not and a lifetime of hearing chatter about such relationships.

That evening, as we parked in the dark alley behind the house, one of the family's sons came out to meet us and guide us inside. In the house were Yasmin, a traditional Druze woman in her 30s, wearing a long skirt, long sleeves and no jewelry or makeup, as tradition dictates; two of her sons, aged about 10 and 11; and Iman, the husband's mother, who lived down the street. Iman was somewhere in her 60s and, unusually for Israeli Druze, spoke absolutely no Hebrew.

Most Druze speak excellent Hebrew, but among the older generation, especially the women who grew up seldom leaving their villages and having no interactions outside the village, some speak only Arabic.

So there we were, the mother, the grandmother, two young boys and two interviewers, one Druze and one Canadian. Deborah has good Hebrew but no Arabic (though some vocabulary overlaps between Hebrew and Arabic, and she sometimes catches partial meanings because of context, gesture and expression and the odd recognized word). The interview unfolded in an organic way, with all six of us (plus the ghostly presence of the absent husband) sitting in the living room conducting an interview in Hebrew, with quite a bit of Arabic. The results would later be not only transcribed and analyzed as an individual interview but reduced, stirred into a pot with other interviews, collectively analyzed and then translated into English for academic writing! Clearly, no matter how earnest our vigilance during the interview and in the discussions and analyses that followed, we would at best achieve an approximation of the complex, personal "truths" of the people in that room.

The interview: six people, three languages. What a mess. What an opportunity. We had pictured interviewing Yasmin alone and then her husband alone, the way our other interviews to this point had been conducted. But since Yasmin's mother-in-law, Iman,[2] was there, and was clearly not going anywhere, we asked her the questions as well.

Picture this: The tape recorder is running (permission to tape received, of course). Yasmin is answering partly in limited Hebrew, for Deborah's benefit, though most answers she addresses to Randa in Arabic. Deborah tries to follow all the threads of the conversation and scribbles unobtrusive notes to herself in English, things to ask Randa later. Iman has no Hebrew at all. Randa is asking her the questions in Arabic, and she is responding in Arabic. The two boys are bouncing about on the floor, their heads moving from side to side as they try to follow the conversation and get a few words of their own in. They do manage to tell us that they both want to become soccer stars and that their greatest hope is that there will be a soccer field in their village. Presently, there is not. The older son tells us later in the discussion that what he really wants is to study and become a doctor. The boys' Hebrew is still almost nonexistent, though they will learn it later in school and in interaction with the larger society as they get older. With each thing that is said in Arabic, Randa turns to Deborah and does a quick translation into Hebrew, so Deborah can follow the conversation and so that there will be a Hebrew tape recording to transcribe. Sometimes Deborah asks follow-up questions, which Randa then asks Yasmin or Iman in Arabic. Deborah tries to read facial expressions and feelings to make up for the blocks of content she is missing. She wonders at the process by which Randa is doing almost simultaneous translation and wonders what will be lost in the process. She wonders about the parts Randa seems not to translate or to condense.

Our interview questions related to identity and aspirations. While our purpose in this book is not to relate detailed findings, we will tell you a few things the two women said in order to give context to our insider-outsider musings and insights.

Yasmin told us (an English translation of the Hebrew summary and translation of what she said in Arabic) that she is

> Yasmin, wife of Jamal. I am from another family, the Har family. I am mother to two sons and two daughters. I am Druze and I keep watch over myself and over the Druze religion. . . . First I take care of my husband, then my children. I watch them closely because of what has happened to our environment [Randa clarified later that this meant drugs entering the community]. I have very strict rules and I invest a lot of energy in them. But first priority is my husband.

This very traditional expression of female self meshed well with Randa's instinct about the absence of Yasmin's husband at the interview. Yasmin lives in one world and her husband in two worlds. Though Yasmin does not live in the past, she deals in her own way with the same conflicts that Randa does, between tradition and the inevitable modern world. She told us that she wants her daughters to continue on to higher education after they finish high school, even though this will distance both them and her from the religion; the girls will not be allowed into the inner religious secrets because they will get driving licenses and study outside the village in mixed company. Yasmin herself will be excluded because of her complicity in her daughter's studies. (Her husband is already excluded by choice; he is not religious.)

Iman, Yasmin's mother-in-law, told us, completely in Arabic:

> I am first of all Druze. I guard Druze tradition. I am mother to ten children, six daughters and four sons. I was widowed four years ago. I live alone now, under the living quarters of one of my other sons. During my whole life I was a housewife and I also worked the land. I helped pay the bills this way. . . . I made sure all ten of my children finished high school. Five got university degrees. It always bothered me that I could not read or write, and I was determined that my children would.

She said much more than this, and Randa worked furiously to listen, interact and respond and, at the same time, summarize and translate into Hebrew for Deborah.

One particular part of this section of the interview is especially noteworthy. When we asked about the future of the Druze community, a long, lively, spontaneous discussion in Arabic began between Yasmin and Iman, with Randa adding a few comments of her own. Randa did not do any summary or translation of this discussion. She listened and even participated to some extent, and Deborah sat in silence, not knowing what was going on. Deborah's assumption was that the women had gone off topic, that what they were saying was tangential to the subject of their research. Only when we were listening to the tape later did it strike Deborah how much remained untranslated, thus excluding her. Only when she specifically asked about this material did Randa begin to summarize the discussion, the gist of which was as follows.

There are people who want to destroy the beauty of the Druze community, to reveal the deep secrets that must never be revealed except to those in the inner religious circle, to those who follow all the rules. Among these people are "evil Druze" from Syria and Lebanon who are publishing parts of the secret, sacred texts on the internet. Nobody knows why they are doing this.

Randa explained that reproducing any part of these texts is forbidden. They may not be published, only reproduced by hand. To publish them on the internet is beyond forbidden. This is shocking and sacrilegious to an almost unspeakable degree; it threatens the very foundations of the Druze religion, and thus the survival of the Druze community, which is struggling to protect itself while at the same time finding its way to being part of the modern world.

On researcher instinct

This incident – the non-translation of Yasmin and Iman's discussion and Randa's initial unquestioned instinct to pass over it – became a milestone in our understanding of one another and our research processes. Deborah became more keenly aware than she had been in other interviews how these stories are Randa's stories as well. Randa discovered another aspect of her instinct: the instinct to protect her community and to not reveal everything. Publication of sacred texts on the internet was so shocking and painful that the depths of these feelings, and their deep significance, could simply never be described to an outsider. One part of this pain is the sense of betrayal by these Druze in other countries. The Druze are one people, one extended clan, wherever they live. How could some of them shake the very foundations of the values they share, the values that have sustained them through the centuries?

We have spoken in this chapter about two instincts of the insider researcher during this particular interview. Let us look at each. One was Randa's instinct as to why the busy, worldly husband did not show up for the interview as he had agreed to do. This instinct was based on insider knowledge of the chemistry of Druze marriages in which the husband is worldly and the wife is cloistered and traditional. We cannot know if this particular instinct was correct, because we never did speak to the husband, and if we had, he would probably not have agreed with this explanation anyway. If Randa's instinct was correct, the husband was likely trying to be all things to all people: polite to Randa, protective of his wife (and mother) and protective of his own way of life, working in the busy world and living in the traditional village.

The second instinct was Randa's urge not to reveal the content of what had been a very personal and painful discussion between Yasmin and Iman, which was not meant for an outsider's ears. So where is the outsider in this? When the two researchers were listening to the tape of this complicated interview, it was Deborah's outsider instinct that the untranslated section did have significance. And so she asked. The unfolding of this – the non-translation, the request for translation, Randa's courage in explaining the painful feelings about the material and what it meant – was extremely important for our partnership and sharpened for us the levels of trust that are required for our work to succeed. It took Deborah several years of working with Randa to trust her own, outsider instincts. In our early work together, Deborah's default position was that the insider's judgment and insight were always right and were the only legitimate sources of knowledge. Writing about this now brings into relief the notion of researcher instinct. Researcher instincts are a kind of tacit knowledge. They cannot be called findings or even data. They are not based on things specifically seen or heard during data collection. Insider instincts are based in lived experience of a culture and are a significant part of the interpretive process, filling in spaces between items of data and sometimes suggesting avenues for further study. Outsider instincts are harder to pin down. They may be based in previous research experience, in personal, parallel experience and in knowledge of (in our case) one another, when two partners are engaged in collaborative work. Instinct is important, and it is real. Nevertheless, instinct should be understood as different from data. One central role of the outsider is to probe insider instincts, to uncover their basis as far as possible and lay them out for discussion. This is an important point. If we view insider instincts as tacit knowledge, then part of the task of interpretation is to help the tacit "participate in the process of articulation," to "co-operate with the explicit" (Polanyi 1958, 87). The outsider's questions and probing are part of this process.

Instincts are not really addressed as such in methodological literature, though the concept crops up in discussions of tacit professional knowledge. We feel that it is useful to identify and name *researcher instincts* as such, so that they can be unpacked, followed up on, explained and confirmed or otherwise through tangible data. Researchers should always try to understand their instincts, because they come from somewhere. As well as being useful guides that spring from relevant tacit knowledge, they can also be misguided, springing from irrelevant sources, and wrong instincts need to be unpacked no less than right ones. The researcher whose instincts are misleading him or her may be misled in other important ways; this researcher's own biography may be obscuring the stories of the research participants.

One of powerful aspects of an intimate insider-outsider research partnership is that each partner can be alert to and ask about the other's instincts, asking, why? Why do you think that? Where does that come from? What does it mean to you? How does it fit with other data we are collecting? We wish to stress again that doing this requires significant trust between research partners, trust that is built brick by brick during the unfolding of a working relationship.

That said, there is always more at stake for the insider researcher. This is *her* life, *her* world, *her* people. Research participants' joy, struggles, perceptions, hopes and pain are hers as well. This does not mean (of course) that each person in a culture shares everything with every other person. People are individuals, with their own stories. Just think of your own family and the family whose home we visited in this chapter. Every person is him or herself. But being part of a culture means, according to Geertz (1973), being born into a system of inherited conceptions that shape how a person communicates and develops knowledge about and attitudes toward life. Research into culture means attempting, through listening to individuals' stories, to see and understand these cultural conceptions and the codes that contain them. An insider researcher's epistemic responsibility is to dive deeply into the heart of her culture, and also to separate from it, in order to fashion a communicable truth. She must decide what to protect and what to reveal. The outsider researcher is a partner in this, contributing a different set of questions and instincts and aiding in the fashioning of the story that is finally told. More on this in the next chapter.

Notes

1 Some methodological aspects of this interview are discussed in Court and Abbas, 2013, "Whose Interview Is It, Anyway?" The quotations from Yasmin and Iman produced here also appear in that article.
2 All names are pseudonyms.

Chapter references

Abbas, Randa Khair, and Deborah Court. 2021. *The Israeli Druze Community in Transition: Between Tradition and Modernity*. Newcastle Upon Tyne, UK: Cambridge Scholars Publishing.

Bonjour, Laurence. 1985. *The Structure of Empirical Knowledge*. Cambridge, MA: Harvard University Press.

Code, Lorraine. 2020. *Epistemic Responsibility*, 2nd ed. New York: SUNY Press.

Corlett, J. Angelo. 2008. "Epistemic Responsibility." *International Journal of Philosophical Studies* 16 (2): 179–200. https://doi.org/10.1080/09672550802008625.

Court, Deborah, and Randa Khair Abbas. 2013. "Whose Interview Is It, Anyway? Methodological and Ethical Challenges of Insider-Outsider Research, Multiple Languages and Dual-Researcher Cooperation." *Qualitative Inquiry* 19 (6): 480–88. https://doi.org/10.1177%2F1077800413482102.

Geertz, Clifford. 1973. *The Interpretation of Cultures*. NY: Basic Books.

Lehrer, Keith. 2000. *Theory of Knowledge*, 2nd ed. Boulder, CO: Westview Press.

Origgi, Gloria. 2010. "Epistemic Vigilance and Epistemic Responsibility in the Liquid World of Scientific Publications." *Social Epistemology* 24 (3): 149–59. https://doi.org/10.1080/02691728.2010.499179.

Polanyi, Michael. 1958. *Personal Knowledge: Towards a Post-Critical Philosophy*. Chicago: University of Chicago Press.

5 Ethical issues in insider-outsider research and navigating the jargon jungle

We feel it is appropriate at this stage to pause for a reflective interlude. The purpose of this chapter is to discuss two issues that are relevant to all research, all the time. One of these issues is the continual development of new conceptual names, which goes hand in hand with developments of new research methods or refinements of existing methods, with new research questions and with new theoretical insights. These in turn are linked to societal changes, political developments and enhanced awareness of the relationship between research and society.

The second issue, related to the first, is the ethical dimensions, responsibilities and implications of the work of researchers. In qualitative research, where researchers and participants meet face to face, in-depth and over time, and participants share their personal stories, we must be especially sensitive to other people and, in our search for truth, to do no harm. In insider-outsider research, which is always qualitative, there are added dimensions of sensitivity and responsibility, as well as added potential to arrive at "true" understanding of participants' lives. Why do we say that insider-outsider research is always qualitative? Certainly, researchers could, for instance, construct a questionnaire on the basis of qualitative findings (we have done this), but by definition, the intimate, time-consuming, subjective process of insider-outsider research means talking to participants in a culture and talking to each other, researcher to researcher, about what is seen and heard and how the two partners are understanding these things. This is a qualitative process *par excellence*.

Navigating the jargon jungle

"The limits of my language means the limits of my world," said that crusty old ordinary language philosopher Ludwig Wittgenstein. Our world is composed of language, of named ideas. Language is the human mode of analyzing experience into conceptual units and describing the rules that link them

DOI: 10.4324/9781003268628-6

(Bronowski and Bellugi 1970). Naming an idea allows people to share the idea, conceptualize it further through discussion, think about it in relation to other named ideas and develop complex conceptualizations of related ideas. This is, in fact, one way of viewing theory, as "a set of conceptual constructs that organizes and explains the observable phenomena in a stated domain of interest" (Pickett, Kolasa, and Jones 2007, 62). Without new named ideas, there can be no new theories. In research, leaps forward can be marked by new conceptual names as much as by any other yardstick. New conceptual names lead to the development of new theories, leading to new research methods, new research questions and new ways of understanding and explaining research findings.

And make no mistake about it, the authors of this book like a good conceptual name as much as anyone. Why, we have flaunted concepts rather freely up to this point. But we sometimes feel that in academic discourse, concepts, once named, and the endless discussions and examinations and theorizations that follow, can obscure rather than clarify. Useful concepts, that is, named ideas that shed important light on the research enterprise and on the patterns of peoples' lives, can, through dense discussions, begin to feel like jargon. This is a tricky issue. We will try to tread lightly in this chapter through the ethical field, littered as it is with important ideas and weighty concepts.

We stated early in this volume that "insider" and "outsider" positions are far from black and white and that different kinds of knowledge overlap and produce more nuanced *positionality* than the simple insider-outsider dichotomy suggests. "Positionality" is a term that often comes to light in qualitative research,[1] with researchers laying out the advantages and disadvantages of different positions and situating themselves reflexively in relation to their research participants. In its simplest formulation, insider and outsider positions are clearly delineated, but in fact, as we and many others have pointed out, there are various points of connection and disconnection between researchers and participants, and positionality can shift during the course of a study (Greene 2014).

Positionality theory is related to the earlier standpoint theory, which posits that "different groups have distinct perspectives or views based on cultural and/or power differences" (Kezar 2002, 96). Standpoint theory conceptualizes "the idea that all knowledges are produced from a power position and are a result of lived experiences, [and] aim to offer a more inclusive understanding of social interactions, considering people as knowers, fighting for a vision" (Marques da Silva and Webster 2018, 501). Standpoint is a more theoretical idea, and positionality is a more visceral and personal one. This is clearly connected to research conduct – the choice of research topics and questions, the way data are collected and analyzed – and to research ethics.

If we view positionality as a more personal, field-based extension of the idea of standpoint, we can see that it is intricately tied to researcher reflectivity and to research reflexivity. Positionality "is the practice of a researcher delineating his or her own position in relation to the study, with the implication that this position may influence aspects of the study, such as the data collected or the way in which it is interpreted" (Qin 2016, np). While we may tend to focus on the outsider's positionality when discussing insider-outsider research, and the difficulty of outsiders really understanding another culture, the insider must also be alert. Qin (2016) stresses that the insider must position him or herself by "looking at 'others' (participants) similar to oneself. A researcher needs to be conscious of himself/herself as an intentional agent who researched and wrote about participants' lived experiences from an insider's point of view" (Qin 2016, np). This idea needs continual revisiting in our discussion.

Carling, Erdal, and Ezzati (2014) argue for a nuanced and dynamic approach to positionality and make the important point that positionality is not only a methodological issue but a political one. "The 'outsider' position is sometimes referred to, with colonial connotations, as 'white research into black lives,'" but this is "methodologically simplistic." Nor is the insider untroubled by ethical complexity. As Greene (2014, 4) points out, the insider must be alert to his or her own subjectivity and bias. It is important to take into account the complexities of "intersectionality . . . which underlines the interaction between ethno-national background and other social categories such as gender and class" (Carling, Erdal, and Ezzati 2014, 38).

Intersectionality "involves the study of the ways that race, gender, disability, sexuality, class, age, and other social categories are mutually shaped and interrelated through forces such as colonialism, neoliberalism, geopolitics, and cultural configurations to produce shifting relations of power and oppression" (Rice, Harrison, and Friedman 2019, 409). The term was first brought to the fore by feminist Patricia Collins (Collins 1990). Collins describes Black American women as existing in a "place" where race, gender, class, ethnicity and American Black history intersect and shape these women's consciousness, as well as how they are perceived by others. Intersectionality is a growing and complex field,[2] clearly relevant to insider-outsider research. We do define and describe ourselves and our participants in terms of several categories (e.g., in our studies we might say that a participant is Druze, religious, a woman, married, a mother and grandmother, over 60) and try to understand the intersection of these categories, how they shape the person and our perception of the person, though we can never accomplish this in a complete way. We describe ourselves in the same way when we are looking at the intersections that have shaped us as researchers. We need to be alert to power relations, sometimes subtle, that may affect the ways we define others and ourselves, and the ways we conduct ourselves, as well as to power relations operating within the community we are studying. The trick, it seems to us, is to do this work without getting lost in it. Reflection can become an end in itself, an endless navel-gazing that at some point distracts us from our research purpose.

Regarding positionality, Robertson (2002) calls positionality "a clunky term" that confines us to predefined categories:

> These categories are the "ready to wear" products of an identity politics that has been especially endemic to American universities. Wearing these categories as if self-evident does not reveal but can instead actually obscure one's unique personal history, even as these categories impart an illusion of self-conscious identity formation.
>
> (Robertson 2002, 788)

Identity politics theories can have neo-Marxist, postmodernist or other theoretical bases (Bernstein 2005), but they always attempt to understand power, oppression, status and identity. Both widely championed and widely criticized (for exactly the reason Robertson states earlier that they tend to provide predetermined identity categories),[3] these theories nevertheless provide important ideas because of their connection to *identity*, and, by easy extension, to qualitative research. "What is crucial about the 'identity' of identity politics appears to be the experience of the subject, especially their experience within social structures that generate injustice, and the possibility of a shared and more authentic or self-determined alternative" (Stanford Encyclopedia of Philosophy 2020, np). It is the researcher's task not to get mired down in predefined categories but to listen to what participants are really saying about themselves. Another good reason to do insider-outsider research! Having a partner with whom to discuss and reflect mitigates some of this danger.

Identity politics interwoven with researcher reflectivity, standpoint, positionality and intersectionality becomes not only a mouthful but a brainful. It is unquestionably noble and valuable work, and we need to do it, but it can overwhelm or obscure the fundamental goal of all qualitative research, which is to discover the lived experience of research participants, in order to shed light on their lives and then on all of our lives; on human culture in all its colors. Conceptual complexity can obscure simple human experience. Whew. So many concepts, so little time. In our earnest desire to understand, to reveal and not obscure, to be honest and ethical, to not oppress or dominate or misrepresent, we as a research community create new names for things, and then we study and examine and discuss and theorize those things themselves sometimes to the near exclusion of actually doing research. It's a tricky balance to find.

Ethical issues in insider-outsider research

When we first conceived of this book, we envisioned a chapter in which the two of us traveled together on an imaginary journey to Canada, to study Deborah's culture, with Deborah as the insider and Randa as the outsider. It would be fair to turn the tables, right? But we couldn't quite work out how to do it, even in our imaginations. What would the boundaries of "Deborah's culture" be? Jewish Canadian families? Okay, maybe (though there are other possibilities). How Jewish Canadians deal with keeping religious rules while being part of society? Possibly; that could be part of it. That would be sort of parallel to the Israeli Druze experience. What stories does the modern Orthodox Jew tell him or herself when the boss says, you have to work on Saturday? What to do when the kids start going out and eating nonkosher food with their friends? What compromises do these families make, if any, and what is the price of any compromise? What consequences, in the family, the community and one's own sense of identity, are there for conforming or not? How do people in these families describe what is important in their lives?

Okay, we thought, those stories could be interesting and could in fact shed light on the challenges faced by various communities who are part of a multicultural weave in a society that (in order to be a society) is necessarily structured around a shared timetable, a shared set of behaviors and activities. This imaginary study could juxtapose in interesting ways with our studies of the Druze community in Israel. But would it really be parallel to the studies of the Druze community that we have conducted together? Would Randa really be an outsider? She has been to conferences in North America and Europe; she is no stranger to life outside of Israel. She is part of the academic world. Deborah had never been to a Druze village, except for driving through a couple of towns that are situated on main roads, until she began working with Randa. Randa has many Jewish friends and coworkers. She is familiar with the Jewish calendar and sends out greetings on the Jewish holidays. Deborah had only a dim awareness of the Druze religious and ethnic group until she began working with Randa. If the tables were turned and the researcher positions were reversed through our imagined journey, there might be some interesting results, but the situation would be different, not a simple reversal.

It quickly became clear, anyway, that there was no real point in *imagining* such a study, since we could not exactly see the point other than "turning the tables." The exercise of imagining did raise some provocative questions, though. If we undertook this study, would Deborah have painful secrets about her community to reveal, as Randa does in our work with the Druze? Would she be brave enough, trusting enough, to reveal these secrets, as Randa has been? Would she struggle to both shed light on and to protect her community, as Randa has? It seems to us that Randa has always had more to lose in our work together and that if the tables were turned, Deborah would not be in the same position.

Perhaps this brings us to clearer focus on issues of power, status and the value assigned to different researcher positions and different kinds of knowledge. The challenge is to look at these issues without getting mired down in identity politics and without over-theorizing the profoundly human enterprise of trying to understand one another. A topic not often addressed head-on in methodological writing about insider-outsider research is this: Why is the insider, the one whose culture is studied, virtually always from a culture that is "native," "Indigenous," "traditional" or non-Western? Is it because the Western research enterprise, with its academic journals, universities, terminology and methodologies, is still dominant over other cultures, worldviews and epistemologies? Is it because Western academia sees itself, not necessarily consciously but by default, as the researchers and not the researched? Is it because research is, by definition, part of academia, that the very impulse to study culture comes from that world and that worldview?

We think the simple answer to these complex questions is yes. We don't need to apologize for this. Cultural research has come a long way from the paternalistic study of "savages." The very fact that so much weighty terminology exists around status, power, dominance and hegemony in cultural research speaks of the earnest sincerity of the research community to do no harm.

The ethical issues in insider-outsider research are the same issues that arise in all qualitative research. There are so many ways that we can go wrong as we "make data" (Ellingson and Sotirin 2020). Data are not just lying about, collections of facts and quotations, waiting for us to scoop them up and report them. Geertz told us decades ago that "data are really our own constructions of other peoples' constructions of what they and their compatriots are up to . . . we are already explicating, and worse, explicating explications" (Geertz 1973, 9, quoted in Ellingson and Sotirin 2020). We are always in danger of misrepresenting, of selecting items of data for our analysis that skew participants' experience in a particular way, of seeing participants' experience through our own lens, of using their experience to communicate a particular message that we wish to communicate, of exercising power in our choice of participants and our relationship with them and so forth. Ongoing reflection on our practices, perceptions and positionalities is the best way we have to mitigate these dangers; this reflection, as we noted earlier, can be deeper and more insightful and critical when engaged in by insider-outsider partners than when we work alone.

Ethical issues are, of course, issues of validity as well. When we engage in unethical practices, we are less likely to arrive at valid, trustworthy conclusions. And one last point linking concept-naming and ethics. When we couch our written research in dense language, it becomes exclusionary, available only to a certain academic elite. We may not expect our research participants to read research reports based on the time they spent with us, and most perhaps will not, but it should be possible for them to do so without feeling too excluded by heavy language. Among the many ethical concerns facing researchers, accessibility of the data we "make" should be among them. We suggest that this is another benefit of insider-outsider research, the chance to discuss together not only our findings but also the language in which we communicate them.

Let us leave this discussion with the simplest of precepts. Try earnestly to do no harm. Seek participants' truth. Write about it so that we as a human society may learn more about one another. Be self-critical. Be curious. Be humble. Be brave.

Notes

1 Interestingly, this term has begun to crop up in relation to quantitative research as well, where validity has been assumed to be achieved through proper sampling procedures, with no relation to the position of the researcher. See Jafar, 2018, "What Is Positionality and Should it be Expressed in Quantitative Studies?"
2 See Ange-Matie Hancock, *Intersectionality, An Intellectual History*, 2016, for a very thorough treatment of this topic.
3 "To the extent that identity politics urges mobilization around a single axis, it will put pressure on participants to identify that axis as their defining feature, when in fact they may well understand themselves as integrated selves who cannot be represented so selectively or reductively. Generalizations made about particular social groups in the context of identity politics may also come to have a disciplinary function within the group, not just describing but also dictating the self-understanding that its members should have. Thus, the supposedly liberatory new identity may inhibit autonomy . . . replacing one kind of tyranny with another. Just as dominant groups in the culture at large insist that the marginalized integrate by assimilating to dominant norms, so within some practices of identity politics dominant sub-groups may, in theory and practice, impose their vision of the group's identity onto all its members." *Stanford Encyclopedia of Philosophy*, 2020.

Chapter references

Ange-Matie Hancock. 2016. *Intersectionality, An Intellectual History*. Oxford: Oxford University Press.
Bernstein, Mary. 2005. "Identity Politics." *Annual Review of Sociology* 31: 47–74. https://doi: 10.1146/annurev.soc.29.010202.100054.
Bronowski, J., and Ursula, B. 1970. "Language, Name and Concept." *Science* 168 (3932): 669–73. www.science.org/doi/pdf/10.1126/science.168.3932.669.
Carling, Jordan, Marta Bivand Erdal, and Rojan Ezzati. 2014. "Beyond the Insider-Outsider Divide in Migration Research." *Migration Studies* 2 (1): 36–54. https://doi.org/10.1093/migration/mnt022.

Collins, Patricia Hill. 1990, 2000. *Black Feminist Thought: Knowledge, Consciousness and the Politics of Empowerment.* London and New York: Routledge.

Ellingson, Laura L., and Patty Sotirin. 2020. *Making Data in Qualitative Research.* New York and London: Routledge.

Greene, Melanie. 2014. "On the Inside Looking In: Methodological Insights and Challenges in Conducting Qualitative Insider Research." *The Qualitative Report* 19 (29): 1–13. http://nsuworks.nova.edu/tqr/vol19/iss29/3.

Jafar, Anisa J. N. 2018. "What Is Positionality and Should It Be Expressed in Quantitative Studies?" *Emergency Medical Journal* 35 (5): 323–24. http://dx.doi.org/10.1136/emermed-2017-207158.

Kezar, Adrianna. 2002. "Reconstructing Static Images of Leadership: An Application of Positionality Theory." *Journal of Leadership Studies* 8 (3): 94–109. https://doi.org/10.1177%2F107179190200800308.

Marques da Silva, Sofia, and Joan Parker Webster. 2018. "Positionality and Standpoint." In *The Wiley Handbook of Ethnography and Education*, edited by Dennis Beach, Carl Bagley and Sofia Marques da Silva. Chapter 22, 501–12. Hoboken, NJ: John Wiley and Sons.

Pickett, Steward T. A., Jurek Kolasa, and Clive G. Jones. 2007. *Ecological Understanding: The Nature of Theory and the Theory of Nature*, 2nd ed. Burlington, MA and San Diego, CA: Academic Press.

Qin, Dongxiao. 2016. "Positionality." *The Wiley Blackwell Encyclopedia of Gender and Sexuality Studies*, 2–16. https://doi.org/10.1002/9781118663219.wbegss619.

Rice, Carla, Elisabeth Harrison, and May Friedman. 2019. "Doing Justice to Intersectionality in Research." *Cultural Studies* 19 (6): 409–20. https://doi.org/10.1177%2F1532708619829779.

Robertson, Jennifer. 2002. "Reflexivity Redux: A Pithy Polemic on 'Positionality'." *Anthropology Quarterly* 75 (4): 785–92. www.jstor.org/stable/3318171.

Stanford Encyclopedia of Philosophy. 2020. "Identity Politics." np. https://plato.stanford.edu/entries/identity-politics/.

6 What has gender got to do with it?

Beyond pronouns

Speaking of positionality, two women are writing this book, and there is no question that this has affected our work. The questions we have asked, the research topics we have chosen, the ways we have been received in Druze homes and the things people have revealed to us have clearly been related to our gender. Two men would almost certainly have chosen somewhat different foci, asked somewhat different questions, received different responses and been received differently in Druze homes. And we are certain of this: Should the research topic be Druze men's experience, male researchers would be more likely to gain participants' trust and receive more in-depth responses. Actually, even the word "responses" is misleading. We do not conduct qualitative research in order to get people to answer questions. We "conduct interviews" – posing questions and engaging in conversations – in order to approach understanding of "lived experience of other people and the meaning they make of that experience" (Seidman 2006, 9). Men's lived experience and meanings are no less important than women's. And of course, not everything is related to gender. People relate to one another in a variety of ways and from a variety of shared experiences.

We hope that an insider-outsider pair of male researchers will undertake a study of Druze men's experience. Until now, the relatively small body of research studies on the Druze has focused on their religion, history and culture, in general (Bennett 2006; Bryer 1975; Firro 2011a, 2011b; Halabi and Horenczyk 2020; Obeid 2006; Parsons 2000); on the place of Israeli Druze in Israeli society (Ben-Dor 1976; Firro 2001; Halabi 2014; Kaufman 2016; Nissan 2010); and on Druze women's status and experience (Abbas and Court 2012; Barakat 2021; Falah 2016; Halabi 2015; Weiner-Levi 2006, 2009, 2011; Yehya and Dutta 2010). The only study we found that relates specifically to Druze men is a cross-cultural study of Israeli, Druze, Arab and Jewish young men's future aspirations (Seginer and Halabi 1991).

DOI: 10.4324/9781003268628-7

This in itself is strange. The assumption is (we surmise) that because women in this traditional society have had less power, less voice and fewer opportunities outside the home and are now struggling to move out of traditional roles, it is most important to hear their stories. Fair enough, but men have their own stories, too, their own secrets, their own aspirations, experiences, joys and embarrassments. It would be very interesting to hear men's stories about their experiences of the movement of Druze women out of traditional roles, a social phenomenon that is affecting the family and village lives in many ways.[1] It is unlikely that men's stories would be revealed to or, indeed, understood by, female researchers to the same degree. In parallel, female participants in this very traditional society would not have felt comfortable discussing deep feelings and sometimes painful experiences with male researchers. We feel that gender is a significant element (though not the only one) to be considered when building and developing an insider-outsider partnership that will undertake a particular research study or series of studies. We especially recommend that such partners do undertake a *series* of studies and develop a research program, because trust, courage, rapport and mutual understanding are hard won. They develop over time, through intense, shared work.

What about a male and female partnership? A man and woman conducting the studies we have done would have brought their own chemistry to the research and been received differently in Druze homes, but in our opinion, something would be lost in this combination, since women would be still more likely to be comfortable speaking with women and men with men. Splitting up the partners, so that the woman interviews women and the man interviews men, would not only evaporate most of the benefits of having an insider and an outsider but it would also result in loss of insights gained and questions raised while the partners interview *together*. This is the idea of a research *partnership* rather than individual researchers or a team. Partners are together every step of the way.

We are not obsessed with gender and are not claiming that women should always, every time and in all research, interview women and men should interview men. Of course not. There are other matching criteria that will be more relevant in other studies. In our specific research context, and given Randa's insider understanding of the different rules and the different lived experiences of Druze women at this crucial time in their history, we feel this is important. Randa's insider status has allowed us to build *rapport* with our participants, most especially the women.

The development of rapport between interviewer and participant, the building of trust in order to achieve valid, trustworthy results, has been widely discussed in qualitative research. Matching between interviewer and participant in terms of gender, cultural background, age, professional background and other relevant personal characteristics is widely seen to be important for building rapport while holding on to the essential research value base set out by Oakley (1981) in her seminal article on feminist research. The values Oakley lists are

> the empowerment of participants in research; hearing often silenced voices; minimising the power hierarchy between researcher and participant; encouraging the participant to lead research; equal sharing of opinions, thoughts, and ideas to minimise the exploitation of the participant (by taking their data, while giving nothing in return); and honest, open discussion of the messy, subjective nature of research when writing it up.
>
> (Thwaites 2017, np)

Thwaites, drawing on other methodological writings, says that insider status (meaning shared cultural background) is not enough to build rapport; an intersection of personal characteristics is necessary. Gender and cultural background, she says, are the most powerful combination, although, fascinatingly, this opens up the possibility of "a deviant insider status, suggesting political motives for carrying out the research" (Thwaites 2017, np). Wow. This seems to us to be a little bit harsh, but we get the point. We would phrase it this way. An insider researcher, matched with participants and able to build excellent rapport, may have *altruistic* political motives: to make known the situation of members of his or her own cultural group in order to gather needed resources and support for them, for instance. This is not a negative or destructive motivation, but it may clash at certain points with the search for "pure" research truth.

We feel that the presence of the outsider can bring to light complex motivations and reactions of the insider. The outsider can help the insider examine his or her instinctual understandings. In analysis, the partners work together through the dense forest of individual human stories, including their own.

To be clear: the current Western social movement to replace "he" and "she" with "they," or with some alternate way of self-identifying and of addressing others, in order to respect people's gender choices, is not the issue here and is irrelevant to our discussion. In this very traditional society, no Druze have undergone gender reassignment. There is no revealed, active homosexuality, although it is generally understood (we could not find a reliable reference for this) that homosexuality, whether latent or active, exists in every society. Again, this is not the issue here.

One of the driving forces in our partnership is Randa's life experience as a Druze woman, experience that is profoundly different than that of a Druze man. This has nothing to do with pronouns and is not a value judgement of any gender choices.

Druze men serve in the army, and largely through this experience, they mingle from the age of 18 in Israel's multicultural society. They drive, work and interact with whomever they want, and if they choose to, they can still be religious, allowed to worship and study the secret religious texts in the *hilwa*, as long as they keep basic rules about dress and behavior. Women cannot do any of these things without forfeiting their right to be religious.

One final point is to illustrate the sensitivity of men's stories, what they might be willing to reveal and to whom. In the course of our large study into self-identification and future aspirations among Druze young adults and those of their parents' generation, one of our questions to young people was whether they intended to go to university (for men, this means after their mandatory army service). Most of the young women did express their aspiration for higher education despite the social and religious price they would pay. Some of the young men did not, expressing their plans to marry right after the army, get a job and start a family. It's a practical decision, they said. I want a family, I need money, I need to build a house, I'll be getting married as soon as possible. Next question?

One young man, however, with great embarrassment, revealed a painful secret to Randa. He told her with his face turned away, his body language expressing his embarrassment. He told her in Arabic, clearly not wanting Deborah to know. He planned to get married as soon as he possibly could, he said, because he so much wanted to have sex. Sex is absolutely forbidden outside of marriage, and marriage is allowed only within the Druze community. Getting married is the only way to experience sexual relations. The Druze are a society of great modesty, in dress, language and behavior. This brave young man did not elaborate, and we moved on. In our discussion later, it was clear to Deborah that, like every response given in Arabic and addressed only to Randa, something private had been revealed. In these instances, Randa would decide later what and how to tell Deborah, pulled as she always is between the determined quest for research truth and her deep loyalty to her community. She did translate this brief exchange, and we saw it as a small but important piece of the story of the challenges young Druze people face as they deal with being young and in their prime, being loyal to and upholding the values of the traditional community they love, while at the same time moving forward in the modern world. We assume that young men like this one will find it harder to marry right away as more and more young women want to pursue higher education and delay marriage. Male research partners would almost certainly have been able to probe this area more, discuss it with other young men and pull back the curtain on men's lives in many ways that we were not able to do.

In the remainder of this book, the stories we tell are women's stories. Not because they are more important or more interesting than men's stories but because these stories resonate in Randa's story. It is these stories to which we had access. These are the questions that drive Randa, the questions into which she had the greatest insight and the questions to which we both were drawn.

Empowerment of women and intermingling stories

One of the elements that ran through many of the Druze women's stories was the essential role played by key family figures in supporting young women's quest to break out of traditional expectations that they be stay-at-home wives and mothers. Traditional, religious, stay-at-home Druze women do sometimes help with agriculture or run cottage industries in their villages, helping to sustain their families economically, but they conform to rules about not driving, not leaving the village unless accompanied by a first-degree male relative and wearing extremely modest clothing.

As an aside, we need to make the point that women are not downtrodden in traditional Druze society. They do not have political power, but they are not property; they are in fact respected and even revered. Druze men may have only one wife, not up to four as is permitted in Islam. A marriage may not be imposed upon a woman, and she may divorce her husband if the marriage is unhappy. In many ways, she rules the roost at home. But in order to be fully part of her society, to be admitted to the inner religious secrets and to truly be "a good Druze woman," she must abide by the rules. Weiner-Levi writes that "the honor of a [Druze] family – and especially of its patriarchs – is linked ideologically with female virtue, but it is the men who are obligated to guard such honor" (Weiner-Levi 2011, 128). Men and women are linked together in the sacred task of guarding family honor. Everyone has their roles to play. And regarding the interconnectedness of men and women, we would like to point out once again that any researcher wishing to fully understand Druze society would need to hear the personal stories of both men and women.

The concept of *honor* is key to understanding the rules and codes. When a young woman breaks the rules, she is breaking deeply held structural codes. Without the Druze family, the Druze are nothing; they will disappear in a few generations. These rules, and the codes that embody them, are how they have survived throughout the centuries without a home country, as second-class citizens wherever they live. What an enormous challenge these people face to move into a modern future without losing their roots! What a conundrum for parents who wish to support their daughters' academic ambitions! The future is clear: The Druze can no longer support themselves through agriculture and cottage industries, both men and women need to work outside the home, young women *want* to study and work and society can no longer function without the possibly corrupting influence of the internet and technology. Families that support young women's advancement know the price they are paying for the rewards that will be gained. The depths and implications of this conundrum were understood only at a surface level by Deborah when we began our work together. They became clearer to her as our studies progressed.

Some of the stories we heard told how the goal of studying at university in order to learn and work in a profession, as well as for personal fulfillment, a goal increasingly shared by young Druze women, requires the active support of key family members. This is usually a father, sometimes a mother, sometimes a husband, and in one story we were told, a young married woman received the steadfast support of her mother-in-law. Because of the requirement for absolute loyalty to family and clan, the daughters of traditional society cannot pursue their empowerment alone. They require ongoing support by at least one key figure within the family. The sheikhs make, interpret and uphold the religious and cultural rules, but in a person's personal life, the family is the supreme and influential authority. Self-realization of a woman born and raised in traditional society requires walking the narrow bridge between tradition and modernity. This bridge is shaky and treacherous to walk alone.

In Randa's young life, her father supported her. He saw his daughter's potential, understood her dreams and ambitions and helped her make her way through community censure and criticism. There is no question that Randa's own biography made her sensitive to particular strands and themes in the interviews we conducted with women. The absolute centrality of a family support figure in Druze women's struggles for fulfillment was understood by Deborah, once it was explained to her, but she did not understand it on a visceral level. She is a product of the postwar West, part of a society in which women study and work as a matter of course. We had many discussions about this and other Druze cultural, religious and family codes as we analyzed our interviews, with Randa *stepping back*, in order to explain, and Deborah *seeing in* through Randa's eyes as well as through the words of the women we interviewed.

This sounds so simple as to be obvious, but it is an important point. When the insider understands so much, when so much of the data resonates with personal experience, this experiential insight needs at some point to be pulled back in order to be examined. The outsider, on the other hand, as well as asking questions, needs to come closer to *feeling* the experience, to finding ways in, in order to get some sense of a lived experience that is very different from that in which he or she grew up. This stepping back and moving in can never be done perfectly, of course, but purposefully practicing it allows the creation of a kind of *meeting place* in the middle ground, where shared understandings emerge and analysis is done. This is an essential part of insider-outsider work. The depth and profundity of these family structures was seen but not felt by Deborah and felt but not seen clearly by Randa until she tried to explain them to Deborah. Again, this meeting place, where the insider steps out and the outsider steps in, is the metaphorical "place" where insight dawns.

In one study we conducted, we interviewed three Druze women school principals,[2] still a rarity in Druze schools. These three professional women fought hard for their professional status every step of the way. Randa knew these women personally, traveling as they did in the small circle of professional female educational leaders. She explained to Deborah before the interview with Samiha the role this woman's husband's mother had played. This brought to light the interesting position of the mother-in-law in a Druze family.

A young married woman's mother-in-law assumes a kind of leadership role in the life of her daughter-in-law, in some ways supplanting the mother. The Druze daughter-in-law, as in other Arab families, is expected to help her mother-in-law (Lowenstein and Katz 2000; Weiner-Levi 2011). The mother-in-law can choose to be authoritarian, supervising her daughters-in-law harshly and protecting her family's honor by seeing that these young women in her household do not go astray, or she can use her position to help the other women under her authority, to take responsibility for their well-being. In the case of Samiha, this was an interesting relationship whereby Samiha and her mother-in-law empowered each other. Samiha told us,

> I must tell you about the true support I received from my mother-in-law. My mother-in-law was not aware of her own value. Her husband and her sons underestimated her. My father-in-law told her all the time that she was not a good mother, that she was an unsuccessful woman. I immediately felt the need to empower and support her, and she stood by my side when the time came. I supported her emotionally and practically, and so I strengthened our relationship, and we had an emotional bond. . . . My mother-in-law supported me when I began to study and advance, and when my husband was against me, she stood by me. My husband became very supportive in the end, due to his mother's support and her faith in me.

Even after she had her teaching qualifications, Samiha's road to a principalship was difficult:

> I began my career teaching classes with learning difficulties. At that time, I was not allowed to teach a regular class because I was female and not a male teacher. However, so many parents sent letters to the administration asking for me to be their children's teacher. This empowered me and pushed me to become an excellent educator. The projects I did

with the students received strong acceptance among the villagers and in the region and strengthened the social bonds between students from different villages. That contributed a lot to my reputation and brought me to be a leading candidate to guide teachers in the region. I became a science coordinator. This was at a time when coordination responsibilities were always given to male teachers. A few years later I was asked to become vice principal.

In the case of another principal, Ahlam, both her parents supported her, and her husband's continued protection and encouragement was key.

I could not have done it without family support. Despite community opposition, the support I received was from my husband and my parents. My husband constantly strengthened me and did not let me give up, not even for one moment. This encouragement pulled me up in the difficult times and helped me not give up.

Ahlam's road to professional advancement was also rocky:

I remember the moment very well when the bid was announced for directing the school. The competition was difficult. Nobody wanted me, not the council, not the parents, not the students. They preferred a man. However, in the end my qualifications won out and I obtained this position.

Maysoon also was fortunate to have strong family support to counteract neighbors and extended family members who opposed her studying and then working.

My parents and my family and especially my husband are the ones who supported me and kept saying that I was their pride. I could not have done it without this.

Randa understood what was meant by "community opposition," having been variously admired, ostracized, criticized and shunned as she worked her way through three university degrees and a progression of academic positions. She knew that only men were expected to hold responsible community positions. Deborah could not have begun to understand the small, daily details of these women's struggles and the inner resources required, without Randa filling in her own details, until the stories almost became one story. When Randa's last child was born, she related to Deborah, no women from the community came to cook for her, to help and to welcome the baby. She was exhausted, and she was ignored. The community behaviors and values of welcoming and helping a mother with a new baby are sacrosanct, and this was a stunning and painful rejection, sending a clear message: You have shunned us, so we will shun you.

Randa as a girl had her father's support, and as a married woman, her husband has always supported her. This makes movement forward possible, but it does not make community censure and rejection any less painful. And the family situations are often complex. In Randa's childhood home, her mother was completely traditional and religious, and her father was secular.

> My grandmother was very religious, though, so my father was very comfortable with my mother. I never heard him complain about her religiosity and her traditional dress. He was an important person in the village and in the bank where he worked, and my mother went with him to village and bank events, with Christians and Moslems, and even to Tel Aviv. She would not shake a man's hand, and my father would just say to anyone who put out his hand, "My wife is religious, she doesn't shake hands." We grew up with that, Mom was religious, Dad was secular, they loved and respected each other. And the children were more important than anything.[3]

This particular family chemistry gave Randa both an ardent supporter of her studies, her father, and a dignified example of traditional Druze woman-hood, her mother. Both of these influences are expressed in her life.

Randa, like the other Druze women who study and advance in profes-sions, does not flaunt all the rules, does not reject her community. These women continue to dress modestly, to uphold values of respect for family, to be "good Druze women" in all the ways they can, while pursuing their dreams. This balance was revealed in small details in our study of the three women principals. Samiha's office door, she told us, is always open. This is partly to show teachers, parents and students that she is accessible, but it also demonstrates her adherence to the principle that a Druze woman must never be alone with a man who is not a family member. There is also a large window in Samiha's office, a window that faces in to the school, so that people can see into her office at all times. The offices of the other two principals we interviewed, Maysoon and Ahlam, also had large windows that faced in to the school. Everyone could see, at all times, that they were not alone behind a closed door with a man. All three of these women wore long skirts, no jewelry or makeup and a white scarf around their necks, as a sign of tradition and belonging to the Druze community. They straddle the two worlds as best they can. Maysoon told us,

> I see myself as someone who keeps the values, especially religious ones. In terms of appearance as well, I keep my conservative look, to dress in a way that appropriately matches my role and position. In our

society, they [the sheiks] try to influence us and to frighten us with religious bans. I voluntarily chose not to enter the world of religion, so that I wouldn't be limited. On the other hand, I keep many traditions and customs, and I involve the clergy in the social activities taking place at school and give them the respect required.

Gender is clearly central to these principals' stories and to our understanding of them. Positionality is multifaceted, but we, like many other researchers, find gender to be an axis around which personal stories very often rotate.

As we visited these principals in their schools and heard about their lives and careers, Deborah was struck by Randa's pride in these women, the way they conduct themselves with dignity as they forge their challenging and determined paths. She understood that she was seeing a mirror image of Randa's story and understood Randa's story better because of this. It was very important to Randa to point out to Deborah the small details of dress and behavior that these women steadfastly maintained in order to balance their lives on the bridge – and as the bridge – between tradition and modernity. Seeing Deborah's understanding, Randa's trust in their partnership deepened. Each step we took together on our research path advanced our partnership, our ability to perceive meanings and to communicate our findings.

We will end this chapter with Ahlam's words, which could just as easily be Randa's, the words of a Druze woman who is both liberated and traditional:

> I think endlessly about any decision, behavior and expression beforehand. I do not give up my own development but at the same time I preserve the traditional Druze codes and customs. I know who I am and what my roots are, and I protect my heritage with all my heart and am thankful to God. The one who is free from the inside has no trouble bridging between the two worlds. It requires some concession and much wisdom.

Notes

1 We went looking for articles about men's stories in traditional societies and did not find any research specific to that topic, though there are quite a few such studies of women's stories. This made us curious, and we did a simple search on Google Scholar of "women's stories" (approximately 1,790,000 results) and "men's stories" (619,000). We understand that the traditionally male world of academia is being righted and that women's previously unheard stories are finally being requested and heard. We do feel, though, that a balance of both will shed the most illumination on changing societies.

2 This study is reported in Abbas and Court, "'We Cannot Move Forward Unless We Preserve Our Traditions': Women Principals as Leaders in Traditional Israeli Druze Society," 2012. The quotations from Samiha and Ahlam are from this article.

3 The quote is from an interview with Randa that Deborah conducted, reported in Court and Abbas 2011.

Chapter references

Abbas, Randa, and Deborah Court. 2012. "'We Cannot Move Forward Unless We Preserve Our Traditions': Women Principals as Leaders in Traditional Israeli Druze Society." *Education and Society* 30 (2): 67–82. https://doi.org/10.7459/es/30.2.05.

Barakat, Ebtesam. 2021. "Gender Struggle Within Complex Religious Realities: Druze Women in Israel as a Case Study." *Gender Issues.* Published online, February. https://doi.org/10.1007/s12147-021-09275-6.

Ben-Dor, Gabriel. 1976. "Intellectuals in Israeli Druze Society." *Middle Eastern Studies* 12 (2): 133–58. https://doi.org/10.1080/00263207608700312.

Bennett, Anne. 2006. "Reincarnation, Sect Unity and Identity Among the Druze." *Ethnology* 45 (2): 87–104. Accessed October 5, 2021. https://web.a.ebscohost.com/abstract?direct=true&profile=ehost&scope=site&authtype=crawler&jrnl=0 0141828&AN.

Bryer, David. 1975. "The Origins of the Druze Religion." *Der Islam* 52 (1): 239–62. Accessed October 3, 2021. https://doi.org/10.1515/islm.1975.52.1.47.

Court, Deborah, and Randa Abbas. 2011. "The View from the Bridge: An Israeli Druze Woman as Guardian of Religious Tradition and Agent of Social Change." *The International Journal of Religion and Spirituality in Society* 1 (1): 135–46. https://doi.org/10.18848/2154-8633/CGP/v01i01/50990.

Falah, Janan Faraj. 2016. "The Status of Druze Women in the Druze Religious Law in Comparison to Druze Women's Status in Society." *International Journal of Multidisciplinary Research and Development* 3 (9): 203–6. www.researchgate.net/profile/Janan-Faraj-Falah/publication/308929580.

Firro, Kais. 2011a. "The Druze Faith: Origin, Development and Interpretation." *Arabica* 58 (1): 76–99. https://doi.org/10.1163/157005811X550309.

Firro, Kais. 2011b. "Reshaping Druze Particularism in Israel." *Journal of Palestine Studies* 30 (3): 40–53. https://doi.org/10.1525/jps.2001.30.3.40.

Halabi, Rabah. 2014. "Invention of a Nation: The Druze in Israel." *Journal of African and Asian Studies* 49 (3): 267–81. https://doi.org/10.1177 %2F0021909613485700.

Halabi, Rabah. 2015. "The Faith, the Honor of Women, the Land: The Druze Women in Israel." *Journal of Asian and African Studies* 50 (4): 427–44. https://doi.org/10.1177%2F0021909614533094.

Halabi, Rabah, and Gabriel Horenczyk. 2020. "Reincarnation Beliefs among Israeli Druze and the Construction of a Hard Primordial Identity." *Death Studies* 44 (6): 347–56. https://doi.org/10.1080/07481187.2019.1572674.

Kaufman, Asher. 2016. "Belonging and Continuity: Israeli Druze and Lebanon, 1982–2000." *International Journal of Middle East Studies* 48 (4): 216, 65–654. Accessed October 6, 2021. https://doi.org/10.1017/S0020743816000805.

Lowenstein, Ariela, and Ruth Katz. 2000. "Rural Arab Families Coping with Caregiving." *Cross-Cultural Studies* 30 (1–2): 179–97. https://doi.org/10.1300/J002v30n01_11.

Nissan, Mordechai. 2010. "The Druze in Israel: Questions of Identity, Citizenship, and Patriotism." *The Middle East Journal* 64 (4): 575–96. https://doi.org/10.3751/64.4.14.

Oakley, Ann. 1981. "Interviewing Women: A Contradiction in Terms?" In *Doing Feminist Research*, edited by H. Roberts, 30–61. London: Routledge and Kegan Paul.

Obeid, Anis. 2006. *The Druze and Their Faith in Tawhid.* Syracuse: Syracuse University Press.

Parsons, Laila. 2000. *The Druze Between Palestine and Israel.* London: Palgrave Macmillan.

Seginer, Rachel, and Hoda Halabi. 1991. "Cross-Cultural Variations of Adolescents' Future Orientation: The Case of Israeli Druze Versus Israeli Arab and Jewish Males." *Journal of Cross-Cultural Psychology* 22 (2): 224–37. https://doi.org/10.1177%2F0022022191222004.

Seidman, Irving. 2006. *Interviewing as Qualitative Research.* New York: Teachers College Press.

Thwaites, Rachel. 2017. "(Re)Examining the Feminist Interview: Rapport, Gender 'Matching,' and Emotional Labour." *Frontiers in Sociology,* 10, November. https://doi.org/10.3389/fsoc.2017.00018.

Weiner-Levi, Naomi. 2006. "The Flagbearers: Israeli Druze Women Challenge Traditional Gender Roles." *Anthropology and Education Quarterly* 37 (3). https://doi.org/10.1525/aeq.2006.37.3.217.

Weiner-Levy, Naomi. 2009. "' . . . But It Has Its Price': Cycles of Alienation and Exclusion Among Pioneering Druze Women." *International Journal of Educational Development* 29 (1): 46–59. https://doi.org/10.1016/j.ijedudev.2008.04.005.

Weiner-Levy, Naomi. 2011. "Patriarchs or Feminists? Relations Between Fathers and Trailblazing Daughters in Druze Society." *Journal of Family Communication* 11 (2): 126–47. https://doi.org/10.1080/15267431.2011.554505.

Yehya, Nadine, and Mohan Dutta. 2010. "Health, Religion, and Meaning: A Culture-Centered Study of Druze Women." *Qualitative Health Research* 20 (6): 845–58. https://doi.org/10.1177%2F1049732310362400.

7 May God have mercy on this thing

Religious codes and women's struggle for fulfillment

Time and voice in insider-outsider research

We have mentioned on several occasions in this book how the trust between us developed and deepened over time, making our collaborative research better. When we began researching the Druze community together, we already knew each other fairly well, as advisor and student, then as friends and then, gradually, as colleagues. But it took years for Randa to feel safe enough to reveal, step back from and analyze particularly sensitive and painful aspects of our participants' stories and even, sometimes, to *see* them, because they are a part of her; they intertwine with her story. This is the challenge of the insider: to *see*, and then to reveal and analyze beyond the obvious, or, sometimes, to choose to protect, to stay at a more descriptive level and move on.

It took years for Deborah to shed her Canadian politeness and reserve that sometimes, counterproductively, told her, don't ask, even when her instincts told her that questions needed to be asked. It took years for her to gain confidence in terms of her role, to grow beyond the feeling that the insider always knows best and that Randa should always lead the way in interviews and in analysis, because the culture is hers, the knowledge is hers. It took years for Deborah to work through when to respect the things that Randa might want to keep private, which is surely her right, and when to move slightly beyond both of our comfort zones and ask. This is the challenge of the outsider: to find his or her role, to respect the insider's knowledge while at the same time trusting the instincts that say, this needs probing, this needs to be brought out into the light and discussed.

Insider-outsider research is not (or not only) a technique, not simply a kind of instrumental strategy that enables seeing a culture from the insider's subjective experience and from the outsider's "objective," nonparticipant viewpoint. An insider-outsider partnership is a kind of organic, living relationship that develops through *time*. Rapport, trust, ways of working

DOI: 10.4324/9781003268628-8

together, levels of understanding one another – all these develop through time. This is true of any human relationship. Of course, the partnership has to start somewhere, and there has to be a first study. If the partners work well together, and if they continue to work together and develop a research *program*, then the third and fifth and tenth study will be better, more insightful, leading to new and richer understanding. In addition to the development through time of the relationship between the two partners, knowledge of the culture under study accumulates through time so that previous insights are brought to the next study.

These thoughts got us musing on the place of time in qualitative research. We are not the first to do so. As Sandelowski (1999, 79) tells us, "Temporal concerns are integral to qualitative research." Historical research investigates past time. Phenomenological research studies "lived time," subjective, here-and-now human experience (Van Manen 1990, 101). Ethnography, while it demands intensive and extended time in the field (see Jeffrey and Troman 2004), usually presents its product in a kind of neutral time – themes and categories that cut across people, settings and chronology. Narrative, "in contrast to the traditional scientific image of the stable self . . . foregrounds the eternally changing self in a temporal context . . . If the traditional scientific enterprise mechanizes time, the narrative enterprise humanizes it" (Sandelowski 1999, 80). We will see this in action later in the present chapter, when Hana tells her story.

Tierney (1997) says that qualitative researchers tend either to write the texts of their findings in chronological time (in past or present tense) or to ignore time altogether (he calls this "disjunctive time"), presenting themes without regard to their temporal place in participants' stories.

Tierney also discusses researcher voice.[1] He says that researchers situate themselves in their texts in three ways, as "I," the most active and personal; as "the author/interviewer/researcher," present but a kind of reporter, more passive and less involved; or as invisible, with findings reported in the third person with no researcher apparently present in the telling. The voice researchers choose for themselves is always related to participant voice (the most important of the voices to be heard in a qualitative report). Does researcher voice add clarity to participant voices? Does it drown them out? Does it co-opt or distort them?

We have found that both these ideas, time and voice, are relevant to insider-outsider research and are connected one to the other. Regarding voice, which voice should the researchers use in an insider-outsider research report? Should the researchers be invisible, their findings presented in a passive, unified third person voice? Should they use the unified, active "we"? Might there be times when the separate voices of the insider and outsider, "I" and "I," or researcher names, should be used when the two researchers had different understandings of the data that remained unresolved? We have generally used the unified, active "we," as well as presenting unresolved differences of opinion on the rare occasions these occurred, using our names. Sometimes the insider and the outsider will see things differently, and there is no point in trying always to homogenize the two voices. Differences of opinion are significant, and if the research partners cannot resolve them, it is important that they write about this as part of their "thick description" (Geertz 1973). Revealed differences of researcher opinion can engage the reader in further analysis of the findings (as it were): Maybe if we couldn't quite figure this out, the reader can, if he or she is given enough detail.

The concept of thick description has aged well, becoming a central tenet of how to write up qualitative research. Almost fifty years ago, Geertz explained the need for detailed, "thick" description of a culture under study, in order to bring readers in and help them assess the trustworthiness of the written account of a culture, because, "anthropological writings are themselves interpretations, and second and third order ones to boot. (By definition, only a 'native' makes first order ones: it's his culture.)" (Geertz 1973, 17) [*sic* in terms of the pronoun].

Does this statement by Geertz mean that the insider's interpretations are always "right"? We have stressed throughout this book that just as the outsider may be blinded by his or her lack of experiential knowledge of a culture, the insider may, to some extent, be blinded by exactly that experiential knowledge, unable to see it clearly because it is so close. We cannot look inside our own bodies. The great strength of an insider-outsider research partnership, with gradually deepening trust and rapport over time, is that both these sets of blinders can be overcome, enabling a fuller vision and understanding of a culture that either researcher could achieve alone.

Thick description, we contend, should thus include description of methodology and the paths followed during analysis, as far as possible, especially in insider-outsider research. If there are differing insights of each of the researchers, the readers need to know. This will be expressed through the occasional use of separate voices.

And what about time? In our work together, when analyzing a body of interviews, we sought thematic understandings that captured shared truths while, as much as possible, not violating the integrity of individual stories. This is Tierney's disjunctive time. When presenting the results of individual interviews, as we do later, we follow what we would call a thematic-narrative approach, with the participant taking the lead on how she wants to tell her story. This last sentence is purposely expressed as "she" because our longest and most in-depth interviews, the only ones we have analyzed separately as individual case studies, were all with women.

Another aspect of time is the sense that sometimes, in the midst of a large study, in the midst of the collecting of many stories and the search for overall understandings of a great body of data, time needs to stop. This happened to us when, in the midst of 120 in-depth interviews, the story of Hana[2] made us stop and pay close attention to her voice and to this one story. She really didn't give us a choice.

Ethnography and narrative

So focused were we on making sense of our 120 interviews, conducted over months of intensive work, producing many hundreds of pages of data and funded by the Israeli Ministry of Education, to whom we had a professional responsibility, that Hana's story emerged almost against our will.

We heard a lot of stories, and a lot of stories within stories, during the period of this large study. We listened attentively, we asked and probed, we conducted each interview as a conversation as much as possible, being open to unexpected directions but always being careful to ask each of our open-ended questions before concluding an interview. We saw our work as ethnographic. We were studying culture.

Hana wasn't interested in our questions, though. She had a story to tell, and she was going to tell it. At her pace, in her way, in the order that she chose. It became clear almost immediately that no one had ever asked about Hana's life before. It was as if she was waiting for us to arrive, finally, so she could tell someone her story. Her story went on and on, and at some point, Deborah made signs to Randa that we needed to rein this in. Visions of the hours and hours of transcription that would follow filled Deborah's head, questions about the relevance of so much of what Hana was saying swirling about. Would the researchers have to choose what to transcribe, filtering through the words and vignettes in order to simply survive the process? What would they lose? And they already had a dozen other interviews still to transcribe.

An aside: We always do our own transcriptions. Listening again to an interview is the beginning of analysis. In our large study, the fact that we were dealing with three languages – interviews in Hebrew, asides to Randa in Arabic, writing the final product in English – made this process unusually time consuming.

As we listened to Hana tell her story, with little or no input from us, Randa knew. She knew that Hana needed to tell her whole story and in her own way. She knew that this was an important story, rich and unusual. She knew we should not interrupt or stop the interview until Hana was done. And afterward, she said to Deborah: After the big analysis, the writing of the big report, we need to return to this one story and treat it as an individual case. Randa saw the importance of this one story, and Deborah did not.

And that is what we did; we returned to Hana's story and "listened" to it as a narrative. We are ethnographers, researching culture; Hana's story led us for the first time into the territory of narrative.

Gubrium and Holstein (2008) discuss how narrative can deal with "the personal self and its stories" (242). "The life course is a developing story, riddled with beginnings, false starts, sudden turns, reconceptualizations, recurrent themes and 'nuclear episodes'" (243). Narrative also deals with "the relational self and its stories" (243), "the self in relation to everyday life, in particular, the social interaction and situations through which self-understanding develops" (243). In this way, "stories are viewed as windows on distinctive social worlds" (244). Hana's story was all of these. It was absolutely the story of her life, deeply personal, and it was also relational, shedding light on her family, her work associations, the religious authorities and the whole web of culture in which all of these were embedded.

Ethnographic interviews and narrative interviews are structured and conducted somewhat differently, with ethnographic interviews generally being semi-structured and narrative interviews being much more open-ended. Narrative research aims to explore the life of the individual, and ethnography aims to describe and interpret a culture-sharing group (Creswell and Poth 2016, 104). Clearly, these aims overlap. They overlap even more when a narrative, recorded as part of an ethnographic study, resonates so much with the personal story of an insider researcher.

May God have mercy on this thing

We will tell the story of Hana in some detail because it sheds light on how deeply the insider researcher can resonate with a participant story and what the implications of that are.

At the time of our interview with Hana, a woman of about 65, she had recently retired from her career in education, a long career that had concluded with her serving as the Israel-wide supervisor for all Druze schools. This is a very responsible position, never before filled by a woman.

Hana greeted us at the door and led us immediately to the table, where a full, hot meal had been laid out. Hana's husband had died recently. Her son, daughter-in-law and grandchildren sat down with us at the table, and we all ate and chatted, at which point the family went on about their own business and the three of us retired to the comfortable living room. Hana was covered head to toe in clothing, with only her head uncovered. Randa said later that if Hana went outside, she would cover her head as well. This is the dress of the religious Druze woman.

We started with a few of our initial questions, and then Hana simply began to tell us her life story. She told us about her childhood, her father's support and her mother's opposition to her continuing her education after grade eight, when girls usually left school, and her studying to be a teacher. What follows are excerpts from her very long and detailed story.

> When I left school after eighth grade I stayed at home for two years and I was very depressed. My father decided that I was going to continue studying. I finished my high school somewhere else. He took me every month to the place I was studying, and at the end of each month he would come and bring me home. So no one could say I was traveling alone. His message was, you will study, you will advance. And the whole community was outraged. My father was under a *herem dati* [religious boycott or excommunication] for eight years. He couldn't go to the *hilwa* [house of worship] or to any religious ceremonies. He was a religious man, but he had to give it up. . . . After that I studied to be a teacher. In those days Arab teachers finished maybe grade ten. But my father told me to go to college and get a teaching degree. The whole community rose up against us.

Presenting selected quotes in this way makes the interview seem like it developed as answers to a series of questions we asked. It wasn't. Hana told us her story in a stream-of-consciousness kind of way, not necessarily chronological. She returned a number of times to the theme of her father. While Randa was rapt, involved and attentive, Deborah, after an hour or so, got rather lost in the meandering story and began surreptitiously checking her watch! At some point, Hana told us about her mother:

> She was against me studying, she couldn't stand the *herem dati*. She went to the sheikhs and said, I don't agree, do the *herem dati* only on my husband.

At this point in the interview, Hana turned to Deborah and said,

> You know what a *herem dati* is, right? You are excluded from all religious practices, and when you die the sheikhs at your funeral say, "May God have mercy on **it**" (instead of on him or her) – as if you were not a person. . . . My mother wasn't in control, her husband was, so the sheikhs released her from the *herem dati*.

Deborah by this time did know what a *herem dati* was; the term had come up many times before. But this was the first time she had heard that someone under a *herem dati* was called a thing, instead of a person, at their funeral.

Hana's father remained a constant in her life until she married. He drove her to her first teaching job so that, even though she was already breaking rules, having studied in a mixed teachers' college, she could avoid breaking another one: driving. She married a modern, educated, secular man who did not worry about a *herem dati*. He supported his young wife, but he himself was vilified in his very traditional village, and when they set up house there

> everyone in the village who saw me always said, where are you going? Where is your husband?

Hana went on to tell us how she fought for better conditions for her students in the schools where she taught (her first school had no bathrooms, no windows, and the children had to bring their own chairs). She gradually gained a reputation with the Ministry of Education as determined, a fighter and a dedicated educator. She went to university and completed her bachelor's and then her master's degree. When she was 36, the ministry advertised for a new supervisor for the nationwide Druze education system. Hana applied and got the job, the first woman to hold this position. She was supervisor for more than twenty-five years until she retired.

During her long professional career, driving her own car every day, working in mixed company, married to a secular man, she kept to modest dress and behavior. This part of the story she told directly to Randa, because Hana understood that Randa has faced exactly the same challenges, since she has followed a similar career path.

> My father was very proud, and rightfully so. Only studying! You must study! I don't know where he got that from. There was none of that is his time, or before, ever. He was a religious man, a real man. . . . I grew up in a traditional religious household. My husband did not. After I got married my sister-in-law said, why don't you wear pants? But I never did, I was always in a long skirt, always modest. Like you [nods to Randa]. I wanted to keep our values. What my father asked me to do. He didn't want me to make any mistakes of that kind. I never went out to a café with another girl or with anyone from work. Work meetings I would do only at work. My father wanted me to be an example of what a modest, traditional Druze woman can do and still be part of the modern world.

After we listened, with little input, for something like two hours to Hana's story, she turned to the present, and her difficult and painful decision to give up modern life in order to reclaim her beloved religion.

> I sat at home for a year after taking my pension. I thought. I cried. If a woman drives she cannot be religious. Why? It's stupid! It's just a rule. I need to travel and I have no one to take me places. [Her husband

had died, and her adult son was busy with his own family. A religious woman may be driven only by a first-degree male relative.] I could even travel to advance my religion. But no. It was humiliating. I had to tear up my driver's license in front of the sheikhs, and bring them the letter that showed I had cancelled it. . . . Why did I decide to be religious? I knew it would limit me, but I wanted to know what is in the books, what happens at the religious meetings, what happens in the *hilwa*. The secular woman can't know this. I wanted this knowledge.

After her long, successful, trailblazing career, Hana was hungry to know the secrets of her religion and gave up a great deal in order to be admitted to that knowledge. But she is very angry that despite the growing modernization of her community, in the end the religious ceiling that restricts women has not moved. She says the only way things will change is through education.

No one is interested! . . . The whole system has to change. And the Druze leaders have to wake up! Why should our leaders just be religious men? Where are all of our educated people as leaders? There should be a committee, men, women, religious, secular, to discuss, plan, decide.

Like the three female Druze principals we met in chapter six, and like Randa herself, Hana was a traditional Druze woman excluded from her religion because she chose higher education and a professional career. But she retained, inwardly and outwardly, the essential Druze value of modesty in dress and behavior. This point cannot be stressed enough. These women love their religion and their community. They pay a tremendous price for following their dreams. They do not reject their community; instead, they stay as close as they can, in a kind of antechamber. Some women, like Hana, shed their modern ways toward the end of their lives in order to know the secrets of their religion and in order that the sheikhs not say, "May God have mercy on **this thing**," when they die.

Going deeper

Randa and Deborah have encountered and discussed these issues over many years, their understanding deepening over time: understanding of each other and understanding of Druze culture. Deborah moved further in, seeing, sensing and comprehending more. Not just facts and definitions – like what is a *herem dati* – but *feelings*, the visceral experience of people like Hana, and of Randa herself, and the meaning of events in their life courses. Randa moved out, in a way, to comprehending meanings of cultural codes she had taken for granted because they were part of her life. She also did a kind of moving in, to recognition and expression of pain, her own, and the pain of others with whom she resonates. This has sharpened further for us the role of the outsider – to trust the insider and to ask the right questions at the right time. It has sharpened the courage of the insider to trust the outsider, and to search herself, to reveal her own story as it resonates with others – because this is the source of insider knowledge.

Early in our relationship, when Deborah first began to understand the implications of a *herem dati*, Randa told her that she has her mother's copies of the Druze religious books on a shelf in her house, and she has never opened them, not once. She will not open them, because they are forbidden to her as a nonreligious Druze. "Sometimes I take them out and touch them," she related, "but I will never open them." The depth of the profound love and respect Randa has for the secret knowledge that is in these books, her sadness that she will never have access to this knowledge and her absolute determination to respect the rules forbidding her to read the books have become clearer and clearer to Deborah as the years have passed. During the writing of this chapter, and our return to Hana's story after so many years, Deborah asked Randa if she, like Hana, might herself renounce her modern ways in order to become religious, someday when her career is done. Is she, too, hungry to know the secrets of her religion? To open and read the books left by her mother? Is it important to her, too, that the sheikhs say, "May God have mercy on **her**" when she dies? These are deeply personal questions. Deborah would not have asked them earlier in their partnership. This is what Randa said:

> I will answer you immediately, without thinking and without reservation but with deep pain and some tears. Unfortunately, I will never become religious and do not think about it because I do not believe that I should be led like someone in a herd after people who are basically uneducated and are the ones who navigate things. I will not follow after these people who say that even the voice of a woman is not to be heard in the *hilwa*, and her opinion is not even heard and is not part of decision-making. I will never step down from my academic position and my social position because it is from here that I can *contribute*. From my position I can influence and lead changes to a better place. I will not step away from this and become another religious woman who simply fills a place in the *hilwa* and walks with the herd and must observe rules that she does not believe in and is not part of. It's very difficult for me to deal with this and that's why I follow the rules as much as I can [following rules of modesty in dress and behavior, like Hana; not opening her mother's religious books]. I believe in my religion but

not in the rules that restrict women, and I will never follow the rules that are forced on me.

Wherever I am I will always look for a common discourse, for an interesting and in-depth discourse, meaningful intellectual discussions. Unfortunately, today I am the only one who has reached the highest level in academia [a Druze woman with a Ph.D., head of a large college]. There are very few who have an education and high status both socially and academically. Belonging to the religious sector means for me killing my soul and myself and completely giving up all my principles and beliefs that have directed me all along. No. I will never do it.

Further to this passionate disclosure, Deborah for the first time asked to hear more about what seems to be a terrible, final punishment: being called an "it" or "a thing" on one's deathbed. Are nonreligious men subjected to this, too, she asked, or only nonreligious women? Randa gave this detailed response.

When a Druze woman dies when she was secular or during a period when she was subjected to a *herem dati* even though she was religious (the boycott of a religious woman instantly makes her deathbed punishment the same as that of a lifelong, non-religious secular woman), the sheikhs say "May God have mercy on **it**, or **this thing**," and to her family they say "God will compensate you for this loss," in terms that make it clear the loss is of an object, not a person.

Yes, the same is true of a secular man, but the sheikhs have decreed that because of the importance of protecting and defending the homeland, since the establishment of the State, a Druze soldier or anyone serving in the security services who was killed in the line of duty for the State, receives the deathbed blessing, "May God have mercy on **him**" and is treated during the funeral and also to the family with the same attitude as would be a deceased cleric – with honor and respect, and without regard for religious status.

A *herem dati* can be imposed for what seem to Deborah to be minor infractions. The example Randa gave during this conversation was, if a religious woman or man decides that at their son or daughter's wedding, there will be a musical band (which is forbidden), the sheikhs immediately impose a religious ban on them for a period of time, and they must return to ask the sheikhs for reentry into the bosom of the religion. These people are called "the lost." If they die during the period of the *herem dati*, they will be pronounced "it" at their funeral.

So closely held are the secrets of the religion that if someone commits a very serious act when they are secular (adultery, perhaps), and then they repent and seek to enter the religious circle, they are allowed to do so after a process, but even then they are restricted. They are not allowed to read the religious books themselves, only the books that give interpretations of the actual religious books. In religious gatherings, they are asked to leave the meeting at the moment when the sheikhs decide to read from the religious books.

All of these Randa explained to Deborah, when Deborah asked, all these years after they began their partnership. Vocabulary, concepts and ideas that Deborah had encountered during her work with Randa, understanding their definitions at an intellectual level, gradually developed into her more wholistic understanding of Druze culture and religion and of the lived experience of the people, especially women, who live in this culture. Randa took great risks in revealing the workings of her people, the rules and codes they live by and sometimes try to break from without rejecting them. She took great risks in revealing her own pain, the depth of her feelings and struggles, the difficult choices she has made and will continue to make. She took risks in standing back from her culture in order to better see it. She is also firmly committed to bringing issues like the rules of behavior for women into the light, in the hopes that this will spur change.

Our two separate but parallel sets of learning and development have gradually combined to form a partnership of intense trust. We feel that the heart of insider-outsider research lies here, in this relationship, with partners traveling the research path together, working to understand one another as an inseparable part of working to understand the culture they are studying.

Qualitative research, with all its well-developed methodologies, is reflexive and self-critical by nature. It is a profoundly human enterprise. Insider-outsider research demands constant reflection, discussion and self-examination, as integral parts of data collection and analysis. It is an important member of the qualitative research family.

Notes

1 See Jackson and Mazzei 2009, *Voice in Qualitative Inquiry*, for an excellent compendium of articles on voice in qualitative research.
2 Hana's story is reported in Abbas and Court 2015. The quotations from Hana used in this chapter also appear in that article.

Chapter references

Abbas, Randa Khair, and Deborah Court. 2015. "Two Ethnographic Researchers Embark on a Narrative Journey." *The Qualitative Report* 20 (9): 1448–57. http://nsuworks.nova.edu/tqr/vol20/iss9/4.
Creswell, John W., and Cheryl N. Poth. 2016. *Qualitative Inquiry and Research Design: Choosing Among Five Approaches*, 4th ed. Los Angeles and London: Sage.

Geertz, Clifford. 1973. "The Interpretation of Cultures: Toward an Interpretive Theory of Culture." In *The Interpretation of Cultures: Selected Essays*, edited by Clifford Geertz, 3–36. New York: Basic Books.

Gubrium, Jaber F., and James A. Holstein. 2008. "Narrative Ethnography." In *Handbook of Emergent Methods*, edited by Sharlene Nagy-Hesse Biber and Patricia Leavy, 241–64. New York: The Guilford Press.

Jackson, Alecia Y., and Lisa A. Mazzei. 2009. *Voice in Qualitative Inquiry: Challenging Conventional, Interpretive, and Critical Conceptions in Qualitative Research*. London and New York: Routledge.

Jeffrey, Bob, and Geoff Troman. 2004. "Time for Ethnography." *British Educational Research Journal* 30 (4): 535–48. https://doi.org/10.1080/0141192042000237220.

Sandelowski, Margarete. 1999. "Time and Qualitative Research." *Research in Nursing and Health* 22: 79–87. https://onlinelibrary.wiley.com/doi/epdf/10.1002/.

Tierney, William G. 1997. "Lost in Translation: Time and Voice in Qualitative Research." In *Representation and the Text: Reframing the Narrative Voice*, edited by William G. Tierney and Yvonna S. Lincoln, 23–36. Albany: State University of New York Press.

Van Manen, Max. 1990. *Researching Lived Experience: Human Science for an Action Sensitive Pedagogy*. Albany: State University of New York Press.

8 New perspectives on method and meaning

A brief virtual tour of the research landscape: Why are we doing this?

As we near the end of this book, let us take a step back. Way back. Back to that primeval question: Why do people do research at all? Any kind of research? Like a zoom-out focus on a map of the earth, let us move back and look at the metaphorical landscape of research. Why do human beings do it? Curiosity is our nature, and we love, even need, to learn. That is a given, and it is certainly a primary motivation for all research. Does research actually help us in any way, though? Let's take a lightning look at a few specific fields.

Medical and biological researches clearly have practical aims, as do genetics, immunology and chemistry. We want to know more about how to cure and prevent diseases and find ways to live healthier and better. Look at the stunning amount of research that has gone into developing a vaccine and treatments for COVID-19. Research has given us antibiotics and vaccinations against measles, smallpox and polio. Researchers work night and day to seek treatments for cancer and other diseases. Clearly, this kind of scientific research is essential to our well-being. But what about other fields?

Geology? Well, yes. We want to know how the earth was formed, what secrets the rocks hold, in order to understand the planet we live on, where important ores and minerals lie, how earthquakes work, so that we can shore up buildings and bridges and so forth. Astronomy? Hmm. Endlessly fascinating, but is it practical? The sun and moon affect our weather, our tides. We need to know how. What, you say? Space exploration? Someday we may leave this planet, as miners, explorers and possibly colonists? Okay. Also, maybe we should know if a comet is going to hit us (so we can say goodbye). Mathematics? Obviously. Those who love it love it for its own intrinsic beauty, but also, it's part of all those other sciences.

Okay, so "hard science" does good work and is important to humankind. Now, as we continue our metaphorical tour of the landscape of research,

DOI: 10.4324/9781003268628-9

let us cross the marked but unfenced border, with nary a guard to check our passports, from "hard science," to its adjoining country, the country of qualitative research. We put one foot down on this new land and feel the soil of "soft science" – social science research. Near the border we see citizens of both lands, toiling together in the fields, doing some sort of collaborative work. Interesting. We gaze around at this new country. We discern people, singly, in pairs and groups, hurrying about or meditatively contemplating, observing one another, asking each other questions, engaging in long conversations, thrusting questionnaires at one another. As we move further in to this green country, we see that it is divided into three counties. Signs inform us that these counties are called "county quantitative," "county qualitative" and "county mixed methods." We see people working in the fields in each county and sometimes traveling between them. Beyond the verdant fields, there are cities with large buildings where people sit in front of computers, analyzing data and writing reports. What does it all mean? Who are these tillers of social science soil, and why are they doing it? Why do social science research at all? Is it just curiosity? Can social science research provide practical benefits for humankind, the same way that "hard science" does?

Yes. Social science research clearly has practical implications. When we understand the ways people live and the reasons they do what they do, this can lead to improving and protecting lives and ways of life. If we know about people's cultures, their values, beliefs, habits and social structures, we can better understand the challenges and difficulties that confront them and work on ways to help. This itself is a rocky and treacherous path, though. Who are we to help? What does it mean to "help"? Do we want to change other people? Who are we to do so? The dangers of paternalism and Western ethnocentrism are ever lurking, even in our more enlightened age. This is perhaps one of the starker differences between the goals of "hard" science and social science. Curing or preventing disease really does help; well-meaning outsider tinkering with people's culture may very well not. Nor is "hard science" utterly virtuous; we do not mean to imply that. Both the hard sciences and the social sciences have struggled to overcome confirmatory biases (favoring results that confirm what one expects to find or already believes). "The scientific method is a tool to help people progress toward the truth despite their all-too-human susceptibility to confirmation bias and other errors. Put another way, science is a history of corrected mistakes" (Wood and Nezworski 2005, 657).

Let's put that aside for a minute and simply focus on understanding one another. Knowing how people live, their habits, beliefs and patterns of behavior, is endlessly fascinating, opening windows on cultures, showing us the many ways there are to be human, the differences between us and the many things we share. This may not be obviously practical, but it is an important part of being human. We can learn from one another.

Nor are "hard" and social sciences as rigidly separate as our facetious opening might suggest – the "border" is unguarded, and much collaboration does and should occur. In fact, we are understanding more and more that many of the challenges faced by humanity require interdisciplinary cooperation, which implies mutual respect between practitioners of different disciplines and different research methodologies. "Complex problems faced by our society, such as climate change, are unlikely to be overcome by a single academic discipline" (Urbanska, Huet, and Guimond 2019, n.p.). Climate change is one important current example of the need for interdisciplinary cooperation. Addressing this global problem requires work in geography, climatology and oceanography, to name a few of the component fields, and also in sociology, anthropology, political science and economics. We need to understand people's local beliefs and behaviors regarding resource use, as well as the broad distribution of resources. A central factor in climate change is deforestation in temperate and subtropical areas, caused by the conversion of tropical forests to urban spaces, agricultural or grazing land (Okia 2012). The causes of deforestation are political and economic, and these find their roots in income gaps, the changes modernization has wrought in Indigenous cultures, the insatiable desires of Western cultures for money, resources and grazing land for cattle – the ongoing clash of Indigenous and Western cultures. Clearly, the "hard" and social sciences are intertwined in studying and addressing climate change.

As another example, the COVID crisis prompted calls for interdisciplinary studies between the "hard" medical and health sciences and the social sciences – calls for "physiology, pathology, biochemistry, immunology, virology, microbiology, molecular biology, genetics, preventative medicine and public health" (Wen et al. 2021, 310) to work together with researchers of policy making and aspects of human behavior related to use of public spaces, social distancing, education, behavior in families, religious activities, movement of populations and tourism, among others.

In addition to calls for interdisciplinary cooperation to meet global challenges, we are seeing an increasing number of studies that directly relate "hard" scientific study to cultural study, notably in the area of public health. Penn et al. (2010), for instance, conducted in-depth interviews with grandmothers in South Africa, in order to understand traditional South African beliefs about the causes of childhood genetic disorders, the goal being to advance the notion of genetic counseling among prospective parents. The study concluded with the admonition that genetic counseling practice needs to include a greater focus on cultural issues.

Genetic study of particular groups of people might be construed as a kind of cultural research – a "particular group of people" often means a cultural group. Regarding the Israeli Druze, there have been a number of studies from scientists in the field of molecular genetics (see Leitersdorf et al. 1994; Weiss et al. 2020). Some monogenic disorders (disorders caused by variation in a single gene) have been found to occur with unusual frequency in specific Druze villages in Israel (Weiss et al. 2020). The fact that there *are* unique genetic characteristics of the Israeli Druze says something about the closed nature of this group, which in turn relates to religion, values, beliefs, politics and history.

So where does this get us? In this chapter, we have attempted up to this point to present a simplified version of a complex argument: that "hard" and social sciences are different but that all disciplines, in addition to their intrinsic interest and the drive to discover new knowledge, ultimately aim to better human life and that interdisciplinary cooperation is often called on to advance this grand, shared aim. Interdisciplinary cooperation implies methodological flexibility as well.

Let's continue zooming in. We are situated now in the land of social science, in "county qualitative." As our vision attunes to finer and finer detail, we begin to perceive separate settlements: ethnography, narrative, case study, phenomenology and others. Again, the borders between these settlements are not fenced or guarded. Some citizens retain residences in more than one settlement and move freely back and forth. In fact, there is a triangle where ethnography, narrative, phenomenology and case study intersect. Within this triangle, we see a small neighborhood. We read the sign at the tree-lined street leading to the neighborhood. It says, "Welcome to Insider-Outsider Research." (Perhaps if we peek in one particular window, we will see two women writing this book!)

New perspectives on method and meaning in insider-outsider research

Insider-outsider research carries aspects of ethnography, narrative, phenomenology and case study. Researchers may certainly define their work as one or the other "type" – we have always identified as ethnographers – but there is no question that studying culture means, among other things, collecting narratives. It means that understanding participants' lived experience (phenomenology) is a central goal and that in order to do "naturalistic generalization" and find theoretical explanations for our findings, we treat our participants and their culture as a kind of case. And while there may be studies where the use of some statistical tool is relevant, insider-outsider research itself is never quantitative. Rather, it is profoundly qualitative, because it seeks, through the unique and intimate pairing of two researchers, to reach the heart of a person or a people, to listen and hear, to feel; to decode, reveal, respect and relate people's stories, helped by the holistic perspective provided by the merging of the insider's and the outsider's understanding. This holistic understanding is greater than the sum of its parts. In this little qualitative corner of the grand research landscape, through method that is learned, developed, practiced and refined over time, new meanings emerge.

Much of the current literature on insider-outsider research challenges the bold distinction between insider and outsider. Some of this literature explores the shifting insider-outsider status of a *single* researcher, especially one who researches his or her own workplace, or who shares cultural background with participants, but is removed geographically and/or by one generation from the people s/he is studying (e.g., Parikh 2020, 437). In the case of research *partners*, an insider and an outsider, we agree to a point that positions are not written in stone. We said at the beginning of this book that there are many kinds of status and experience, many kinds of positionality. In our work, Deborah found herself at least a partial insider, sharing experiences as a woman, a mother and an educator, in conversations with our participants. She also learned more and more about the Druze as the years of our studies progressed and is certainly now less ignorant of Druze culture than she was at the beginning. An outsider may have many points of connections with participants.

As Couture, Zaidi, and Maticka-Tyndale (2012, 86) explain, "intersecting identities and resulting insider/outsider status" may influence the data collection phase of a study regarding culturally and religiously sensitive issues. Couture, Zaidi and Maticka-Tyndale used "an intersectional approach to explore the fluidity of [their] insider/outsider statuses resulting from multiple and intersecting identities such as ethnicity, religion, age, and sex. The multiple identities a researcher possesses can cause him/her to be perceived as an insider and outsider simultaneously, which can play a significant role in shaping the interactions between the interviewer and interviewee." While there is no question that this is true, in our research we remain firm in our self-definitions as an insider and an outsider. Points of commonality may both help and confuse the outsider's attempts to understand participants' lived experience. As in all qualitative research, reflection on developing insights requires ongoing self-questioning. Where did this insight originate? Does it come from participants' stories, from the data or from my experience? Am I missing something? Are there cultural norms and codes here that I have failed to comprehend? The power of insider-outsider research is that the outsider has a partner with whom to work through these questions.

Despite the somewhat shifting positionality and the sharing with participants of various points of experience, Deborah *will always be an outsider to*

Druze culture. She did not grow up Druze or live with Druze, and she does not speak Arabic. She shares no visceral, lived experience of being Druze. We want to underscore this point.

Randa, the insider, experiences some level of outsiderness as a professional, academic woman who does not fit the traditional mold of the Druze woman. Nevertheless, she is Druze. The insider's challenge is, paradoxically, to ask the same questions as the outsider: Where did this insight originate? Does it come from participants' stories, from the data or from my experience? Am I missing something? Are there cultural norms and codes here that I have failed to comprehend?

Why might an insider fail to comprehend cultural codes? Because they are too near, they are a part of the insider's very being. The power of insider-outsider research is that there is a partner with whom to work through these questions! The insider's reflective process is parallel to but different from that of the outsider. "It is critical to articulate a researcher's positionality as an 'insider' by looking at 'others' (participants) similar to oneself. A researcher needs to be conscious of himself/herself as an intentional agent who researched and wrote about participants' lived experiences from an insider's point of view"(Qin 2016, np). This is indeed a challenge: to be Druze, welcomed into Druze homes, speaking the native tongue as well as the language of culture, religion and shared experience; to delve deep into self-understanding in order to understand participants' experience; and also to step back, to say, this is *like* my story in many ways, but it is not my story.

We have no argument with Savvides et al. (2014) that constant critical reflexivity on the part of both researchers to "consider and make transparent how their positionality impacts on the entire research process" (412) is essential.

Randa has a complex and sometimes shifting positionality in relation to her community. She grew up Druze, in a Druze family, and she identifies proudly as Druze. But she has forged an unusual professional and academic path, suffering resentment, criticism and distancing as a result of this. She interacts at a national and international level with people in the academic world. Despite this, she shares with participants the visceral, lived experience of being Druze, *and she will always be an insider to Druze culture.*

Understanding and respecting the notion of positionality, we remain convinced that, in our research and from our experience, we are an insider and an outsider to Druze culture.

Theory and meaning

We, the research community, can try so earnestly to be fair, to analyze, to theorize and conceptualize, that we may sometimes get lost in a dense forest of concepts and terminology. It would seem, for instance, that intersectionality would be a useful analytic framework to understand the experience of Druze women, "intersectionality" being a primary lens through which to view oppression. The core insight of work in intersectionality is that "in a given society at a given time, power relations of race, class and gender . . . build on each other and work together; and that, while often invisible, these intersecting power relations affect all aspects of the social world" (Collins and Bilge 2020, 2). Understanding and respecting this insightful theoretical contribution, we have not found it useful for our own work. The language is somehow too laden for the human stories we want to tell. And also, imposing this lens on Druze women's stories assumes that they are oppressed. Perhaps they do not all see it quite that way.

Seen from earlier discussion, using our zoom-out lens, great forests of terminology can be seen all over the vast research landscape, in every country, county and neighborhood. The forests may be even denser (it seems to us) in qualitative country, perhaps because we as qualitative researchers still doubt our ability to produce legitimate knowledge, the tangible kind that they produce in "hard" science land. The roots of this lack of self-confidence are

historical. In the mid-and late twentieth century, qualitative research was juxtaposed to quantitative research, which had made great strides in its sophistication and reach. In response to their increasing marginalization, qualitative researchers spent much of their intellectual energy boosting their credentials. After all, stripped of its methodological dress-up, participant observation looks a lot like hanging out with people, and interviewing like a way to say the researchers had a few conversations. How can such mundane methods compete with inferences based on statistical analysis? . . . The relation among theory, observation and method thus remains an Achilles heel of qualitative research.

(Tavory and Timmermans 2014, 3)

Perhaps we overcompensate by over-theorizing, or at least by over-verbalizing our theorizing. From our perspective, heavily laden language can obscure ground-level human experience. Of course, qualitative researchers cannot remain at the level of description. Of course, we cannot simply provide endless quotations and expect the readers to make sense of the story themselves. "The fundamental question organizing all data analysis – 'what is this a case of?' – is a semiotic question: a question of the ongoing construction of meaning" (Tavory and Timmermans 2014, 5). We seek to arrive at understanding of *participants' meanings* through our in-depth participant observations and interviews, and then we attempt to derive more general, generalizable meaning from the details of our data by theorizing. It's a tricky job, theorizing while never forgetting that our work is a profoundly human enterprise. It is about people and their lives.

We have mentioned epistemic responsibility in this book, and here we should address it once more. The idea of epistemic responsibility is rooted in the old philosophical question: How do you know? Traditional epistemology says that we can claim to "know" something on the basis of "justified true belief." In research, we might say that justified true belief – in effect, the trustworthiness of our research findings and claims – is rooted in careful data collection and analysis. Code (2020, x) quotes a classic 1983 essay by Kornblith, who suggests that "when someone wonders whether a belief is *justified* she/he is asking whether the belief is the product of *epistemically responsible action* taken by an *epistemically responsible agent.*" This is clearly and directly relevant to research.

Producing "true" or trustworthy knowledge about a people and their culture requires sensitive, patient, attentive listening to stories, as well as observations of people going about their lives, and then painstakingly attempting to rise above the details to attain more general understanding. A rush to theorize, to explain people's lives with heavy conceptual language, may obscure, may not be true to those people's lived experience and thus may be, unintentionally, *epistemically irresponsible.*

The task is great, because from our patient, attentive listening, we wish to discern cultural codes and their meanings in the lives of people in the culture we are studying. Once again recognizing the out-of-date pronouns, we ground ourselves in the qualitative research task as Malinowski envisioned it, all those years ago: "the real work of anthropology: to grasp the native's point of view, *his* relation to life, to realize *his* vision, *his* world." We have to be careful that in our theorizing, and in our coining and applying of new concepts, we do not get lost in a conceptual forest, losing participants' meaning and mistakenly imposing our own.

Dear reader, imagine once again that zoom lens. Its focus starts in the clouds, high above the earth. It moves down through the clouds to our first view of the vast research landscape, with its mountains, rivers and valleys, closer, closer, beyond "hard" science country to social science land and then, closer still, to county qualitative. We begin to see people working in the fields. We zoom in more to smaller settlements and finally to the Insider-Outsider Research neighborhood. This time we do peek in the window of one particular house, and there we see Randa and Deborah, engaged in vibrant, earnest conversation about the people who have shared their stories, the meanings of those stories and the codes that they reveal and how various stories might fit together into "true" accounts of Druze culture.

Why have you wanted, all these years, to study Druze culture? Deborah asks Randa. Because I love my culture and my religion, Randa answers.

I want the world to know about it. I want my people to move forward while never forsaking their hearts and souls. I want to share our story with people in other traditional cultures, especially with women who want to move forward while holding fast to their roots.

And why did you want to take your research journey with me? Deborah asks, humbled and grateful to share the journey. Because, Randa answers, with you I saw and understood things I could not quite see and understand alone, because they are too near. Because neither I nor you alone could have seen and understood these things in the same ways. Because I did not quite know how to communicate these insights to people who do not know the Druze. And because people need friends on their journeys.

Randa turns to Deborah and asks, somewhat to Deborah's surprise, why did you want to walk with me on this journey? It takes a minute for Deborah to search for the answer and to formulate it clearly. Because I saw something in you from the beginning, she says, a light and curiosity and passion. Because, once we began, I began to see the beauty and uniqueness and secrets of the Druze and how your religion, culture and history have shaped each other. I can say now, almost twenty years in, that taking this journey with you has brought me to understandings of culture and of qualitative research at which I would never have otherwise arrived. I thank you for that. And I wanted to walk with you because people need friends on their journeys.

We believe that the best chance of approaching "true" understandings of a culture is with an insider and an outsider researcher, working together in a genuine *partnership* that develops over time, and is built, slowly, on trust, discussion, listening, patience, rapport, courage, on-going examination of insider and outsider instincts and deep mutual respect.

Best wishes on your journeys.

Chapter references

Code, Lorraine. 2020. *Epistemic Responsibility*, 2nd ed. New York: Suny Press.

Collins, Patricia Hill, and Sirma Bilge. 2020. *Intersectionality*, 2nd ed. Cambridge, UK: Polity Press.

Couture, Amanda L., Arshia U. Zaidi, and Eleanor Maticka-Tyndale. 2012. "Reflexive Accounts: An Intersectional Approach to Exploring the Fluidity of Insider-Outsider Status and the Researcher's Impact on Culturally Sensitive Post-Positive Qualitative Research." *Qualitative Sociology Review* 8 (1): 86–105. http://qsr.webd.pl/ENG/Volume21/QSR_8_1_Couture_Zaidi_Maticka-Tyndale.pdf.

Kornblith, Hilary. 1983. "Justified Belief and Epistemically Responsible Action." *Philosophical Review* 92 (1): 33–48. www.jstor.org/stable/2184518.

Leitersdorf, Eran, Rifaat Safadi, Vardiella Meiner, Ayeleth Reshef, Ingemar Björkhem, Yechiel Friedlander, Siman Morkos, and Vladimir M. Berginer. 1994. "Cerebrotendinous Xanthomatosis in the Israeli Druze: Molecular Genetics and

Phenotypic Characteristics." *American Journal of Human Genetics* 55 (5): 907–15. www.ncbi.nlm.nih.gov/pmc/articles/PMC1918342/.

Okia, Clement, ed. 2012. *Global Perspectives on Sustainable Forest Management.* Rijeka, Croatia: InTech.

Parikh, Aparna. 2020. "Insider-Outsider as Process: Drawing as Reflexive Feminist Methodology During Fieldwork." *Cultural Geographies* 27 (3): 437–52. https://doi.org/10.1177%2F1474474019887755.

Penn, Claire, Jennifer Watermeyer, Carol MacDonald, and Colleen Moabelo. 2010. "Grandmothers as Gems of Genetic Wisdom: Exploring South African Traditional Beliefs About the Causes of Childhood Genetic Disorders." *Journal of Genetic Counseling* 19: 9–21. https://doi.org/10.1007/s10897-009-9252-x.

Qin, Donxiao. 2016. "Positionality." *The Wiley-Blackwell Encyclopedia of Gender and Sexuality Studies.* https://doi.org/10.1002/9781118663219.wbegss619.

Savvides, Nicola, Joanna Al-Youseff, Mindy Colin, and Cecilia Garrido. 2014. "Journeys into Inner/Outer Space: Reflections on the Methodological Challenges of Negotiating Insider/Outsider Status in International Educational Research." *Research in Comparative and International Education* 9 (4): 412–25. https://doi.org/10.2304%2Frcie.2014.9.4.412.

Tavory, Iddo, and Stefan Timmermans. 2014. *Abductive Analysis: Theorizing Qualitative Research.* Chicago: University of Chicago Press.

Urbanska, Karolina, Sylvie Huet, and Serge Guimond. 2019. "Does Increased Interdisciplinary Contact Among Hard and Social Scientists Help or Hinder Interdisciplinary Research?" *Plos One*, published on-line September 4. https://doi.org/10.1371/journal.pone.0221907.

Weiss, Karin, Nina Ekhilevich, Lior Cohen, Sharon Bratman-Morag, Rachel Bello, Ariel Martinez, Yarin Hadid, Liran Shlush, Alina Kurolap, Tamar Paperna, Adina Mory, Hagit Baris, and Maximilian Muenke. 2020. "Identification of a Novel PCNT Founder Pathogenic Variant in the Israeli Druze Population." *European Journal of Medical Genetics* 63 (2). Article 103643. https://doi.org/10.1016/j.ejmg.2019.03.007.

Wen, Jun, Wei Wang, Metin Kozak, Xinyi Liu, and Haifeng Hou. 2021. "Many Brains Are Better Than One: The Importance of Interdisciplinary Studies on Covid-19 in and Beyond Tourism." *Tourism Recreation Research* 46 (2): 310–13. https://doi.org/10.1080/02508281.2020.1761120.

Wood, James M., and M. Teresa Nezworski. 2005. "Science as a History of Corrected Mistakes: Comment." *American Psychologist* 60 (6): 657–58. https://psycnet.apa.org/doi/10.1037/0003-066X.60.6.657.

Index

Banks, James 9
Boas, Franz 5

concepts 38
cultural codes 21, 24–5, 74
culture 5, 22, 71, 72

Druze religion 15–16, 24

educational ethnography 10
emic 7
epistemic responsibility 30–1, 36, 76
epistemological privilege 9
ethics 22, 38, 41, 42, 43
ethnographic interview 61
ethnography 7–8, 60
etic 7

Geertz, Clifford 22, 36, 59
gender 45–8

"hard science" 70–2
herem dati 62, 63, 65, 66
hilwa 48, 64, 65

identity politics 40
IDF (Israel Defense Forces) 26
intersectionality 40, 75

jargon 38

knowledge 30

Malinowski, Bronislaw 5–6
Mead, Margaret 10

narrative 60, 61
narrative interview 61

participant observation 5
Pike, Kenneth 7
positionality 38–40, 74
post-modernism 7

reflectivity 8
reflexivity 8
researcher instinct 34–5
Ruby, Jay 9

social science research 70–2
standpoint theory 38

theory 38, 74–5
thick description 59
time 58–60
trust 27, 30

urban anthropology 10

validity 43
voice 59–60

For Product Safety Concerns and Information please contact our EU
representative GPSR@taylorandfrancis.com
Taylor & Francis Verlag GmbH, Kaufingerstraße 24, 80331 München, Germany